2012 上半年
First Half of 2012

中国国际收支报告
China's Balance of Payments Report

国家外汇管理局国际收支分析小组
BOP Analysis Group
State Administration of Foreign Exchange

中国金融出版社
CHINA FINANCIAL PUBLISHING HOUSE

责任编辑：张翠华　马　杰
责任校对：刘　明
责任印制：程　颖

图书在版编目（CIP）数据

2012 上半年中国国际收支报告（2012 Shangbannian Zhongguo Guoji Shouzhi Baogao）/国家外汇管理局国际收支分析小组编．—北京：中国金融出版社，2013.1
ISBN 978-7-5049-6732-9

Ⅰ．①2… Ⅱ．①国… Ⅲ．①国际收支—研究报告—中国—2012 Ⅳ．①F812.4

中国版本图书馆 CIP 数据核字（2013）第 014811 号

出版
发行　中国金融出版社
社址　北京市丰台区益泽路 2 号
市场开发部　（010）63266347，63805472，63439533（传真）
网上书店　http://www.chinafph.com　（010）63286832，63365686（传真）
读者服务部　（010）66070833，62568380
邮编　100071
经销　新华书店
印刷　天津银博印刷技术发展有限公司
尺寸　210 毫米 ×285 毫米
印张　9.75
字数　185 千
版次　2013 年 1 月第 1 版
印次　2013 年 1 月第 1 次印刷
印数　1—2000
定价　80.00 元
ISBN 978-7-5049-6732-9/F.6292

国家外汇管理局
国际收支分析小组人员名单

组　　长：易　纲
副 组 长：邓先宏　方上浦　王小奕　李　超　杨国中　黄国波
审　　稿：刘　薇　杜　鹏　孙鲁军　王允贵　王春英　崔汉忠
统　　稿：管　涛　方　文　温建东　周　济
执　　笔：
第一部分：王彩玲　马　昀　管恩杰　赵玉超
第二部分：孙刚强　李玲青　吴　昊　陈之平　马玉娟
第三部分：贾　宁　龙　芳
第四部分：王彩玲　马　昀
专　　栏：谢月兰　赵玉超　温建东　陈志刚　贾　宁　王彩玲

附录整理：卞　强
英文翻译：周海文　王　亮　胡　红
英文审校：Nancy Hearst（美国哈佛大学费正清东亚研究中心）

Contributors to This Report

Head
Yi Gang

Deputy Head
Deng Xianhong   Fang Shangpu   Wang Xiaoyi   Li Chao
Yang Guozhong   Huang Guobo

Readers
Liu Wei   Du Peng   Sun Lujun   Wang Yungui   Wang Chunying
Cui Hanzhong

Editors
Guan Tao   Fang Wen   Wen Jiandong   Zhou Ji

Authors
Part One: Wang Cailing   Ma Yun   Guan Enjie   Zhao Yuchao
Part Two: Sun Gangqiang   Li Lingqing   Wu Hao   Chen Zhiping
Ma Yujuan
Part Three: Jia Ning   Long Fang
Part Four: Wang Cailing   Ma Yun
Boxes: Xie Yuelan   Zhao Yuchao   Wen Jiandong   Chen Zhigang
Jia Ning   Wang Cailing

Appendix: Bian Qiang

Translators: Zhou Haiwen   Wang Liang   Hu Hong

Proofreader: Nancy Hearst (Fairbank Center for East Asian Research, Harvard University)

内容摘要

2012 年上半年，全球经济增长放缓，国际金融持续动荡，大宗商品价格大幅波动，新兴市场普遍出现资本外流。我国加强和改进宏观调控，进一步促进国际收支基本平衡，国内经济缓中趋稳，金融支持实体经济的力度加大，人民币汇率逐步趋近合理均衡水平，但稳定经济增长和化解金融风险的任务依然艰巨。

在复杂严峻的国内外因素影响下，2012 年上半年，我国涉外经济活动保持平稳增长，国际收支交易总规模同比增长 10%。国际收支趋向更加平衡，经常项目顺差 772 亿美元，资本和金融项目顺差 149 亿美元，同比分别下降 12% 和 92%；经常项目顺差与国内生产总值之比为 2.1%，较 2011 年同期下降 0.7 个百分点；国际收支口径的外汇储备增加 636 亿美元（剔除汇率和资产价格变动的估值影响），较 2011 年同期少增 2 174 亿美元。跨境资本流动呈现双向变化，2012 年第一季度资本和金融项目由 2011 年第四季度的逆差 290 亿美元转为顺差 561 亿美元，第二季度再现净流出 412 亿美元。

下半年，不稳定、不确定的因素依然较多，但有利于我国国际收支平衡的积极因素正在逐步积累，我国国际收支仍有望保持基本平衡。下一阶段，外汇管理工作将把握好稳中求进的主基调，把稳增长放在更加重要位置，继续促进贸易投资便利化，加快外汇市场发展，坚持防风险不放松，密切跟踪跨境资金流动走势，完善政策预案，进一步提高外汇管理服务实体经济和维护国家经济金融安全的能力。

Abstract

In the first half of 2012 global economic growth slowed down, both international financial markets and bulk commodity prices fluctuated, and the emerging markets experienced widespread capital outflows. China strengthened macro control by improving its balance-of-payments situation, stabilizing domestic economic growth by slowing down growth, and providing more financial support for the real economy. The RMB exchange rate gradually approached a reasonable equilibrium. However, there remained the serious tasks of maintaining steady economic growth and preventing financial risks.

Despite the complex and grim international environment, China's external economic activity maintained steady growth, with the volume of balance-of-payment transactions increasing 10 percent year on year. The balance-of-payments situation tended to be more balanced: the current account and the capital and financial account recorded surpluses of USD 77.2 billion and USD 14.9 billion respectively, down by 12 percent and 92 percent year on year; the ratio of the current account surplus to GDP was 2.1 percent, 0.7 percentage point lower than the ratio during the first half of 2011; foreign reserve assets increased by USD 63.6 billion (excluding the valuation effect of the exchange rate and the asset price), USD 217.4 billion lower than that during the first half of 2011. Cross-border capital flows recorded a two-way fluctuation: the capital and financial account moved from a deficit of USD 29 billion in the fourth quarter of 2011 to a surplus of USD 56.1 billion in the first quarter of 2012, and then returned to a deficit of USD 41.2 billion in the second quarter of 2012.

As forecasted, the balance of payments remained uncertain and unstable, but positive factors were accumulating and China's balance of payments will achieve an equilibrium in the second half of the year. The state administration authority will retain the key tone of steady growth by improving facilitation of trade and investment, accelerating development of the foreign exchange market, guarding against risks, maintaining close monitoring of cross-border capital flows, perfecting foreign exchange policy plans and improving its capability to serve the real economy and maintaining financial security.

目 录

专栏

图

表

Contents

Boxes

Charts

Tables

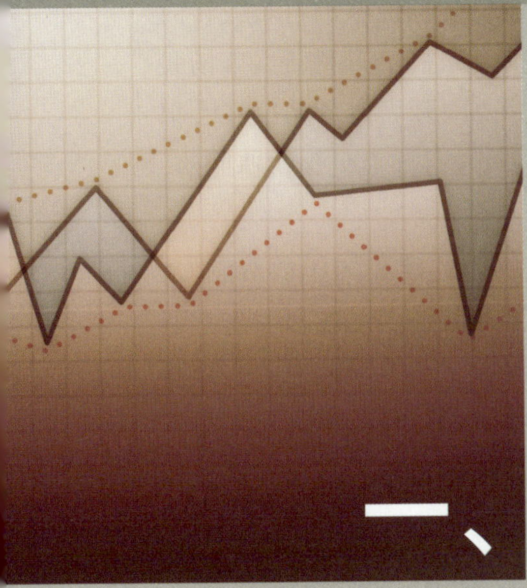

一、国际收支概况

（一）国际收支运行环境

2012年上半年，全球经济增长放缓，发达经济体复苏乏力，特别是欧元区经济增长停滞，主要新兴经济体也呈现增长回落的态势（见图1-1）。国际金融市场持续震荡，第一季度欧债危机有所缓和，但第二季度随着希腊政局动荡、西班牙和意大利主权债务及银行部门等风险加大，欧债危机震荡升级，国际市场避险情绪上升（见图1-2）。新兴经济体普遍面临资本流出压力，大量资金回流欧洲自救或转向安全资产，主要新兴经济体股市和货币出现波动，第二季度摩根士丹利新兴市场股票指数累计下跌10%，货币指数累计下跌5%（见图1-3）。国际大宗商品价格大幅波动，纽约轻质原油期货价格和伦敦金属交易所期铜价格自3月前后见顶快速回落，截至6月末分别下滑21%和12%。

2012年上半年，我国继续坚定不移地扩大国内消费需求，改善居民消费能力，优化投资结构，鼓励民间投资，出台稳出口、扩进口的政策措施，促进国际收支朝着平衡的方向发展。实施积极的财政政策和稳健的货币政策，加大政策预调、微调力度，国内经济缓中趋稳，上半年国内生产总值（GDP）增长7.8%，物价涨幅明显回落（见图1-4），但经济结构调整和稳定经济增长的任务依然艰巨。金融支持经济

图 1-1

2007—2012年上半年主要经济体经济增长率

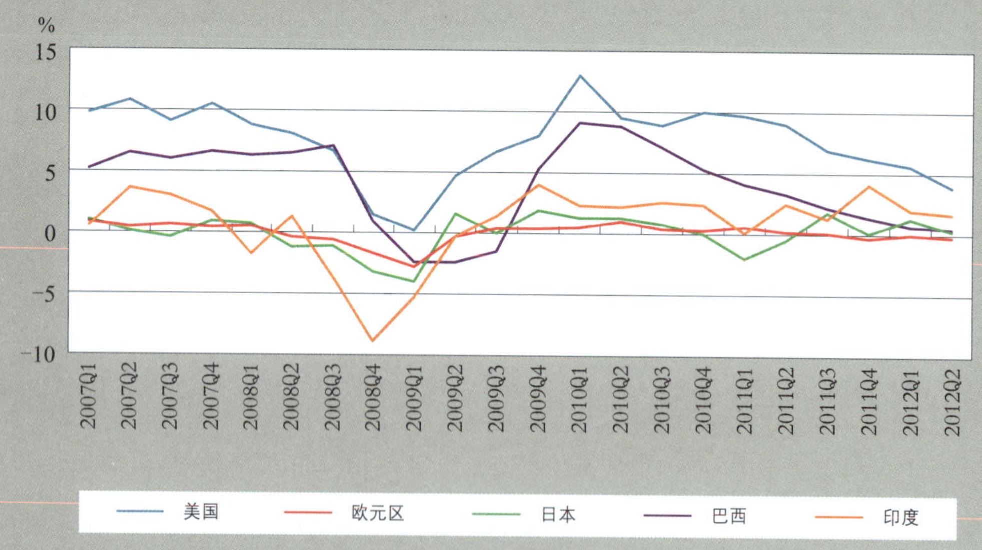

注：美国、欧元区和日本数据为季度环比，巴西和印度数据为季度同比。

数据来源：环亚数据库。

图 1-2

2011—2012 年上半年意大利和西班牙国债 CDS 及市场波动率 VIX 指数

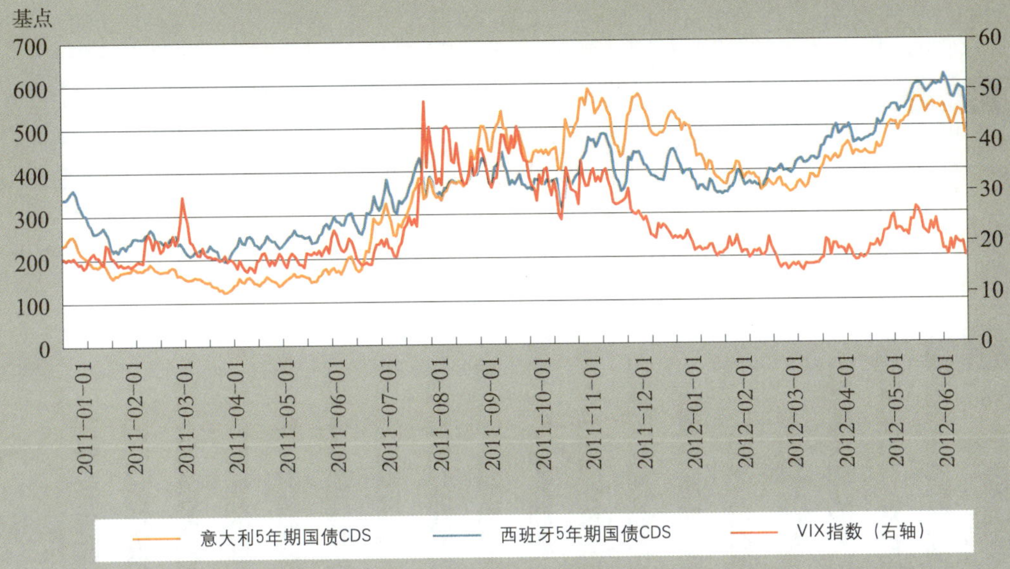

注：CDS（信用违约掉期）价格越高，意味着市场认为信用主体的违约风险越大。市场波动率 VIX 指数越高说明市场恐慌情绪越重。

数据来源：彭博资讯、路透。

图 1-3

2011—2012 年上半年新兴市场股票指数和货币指数

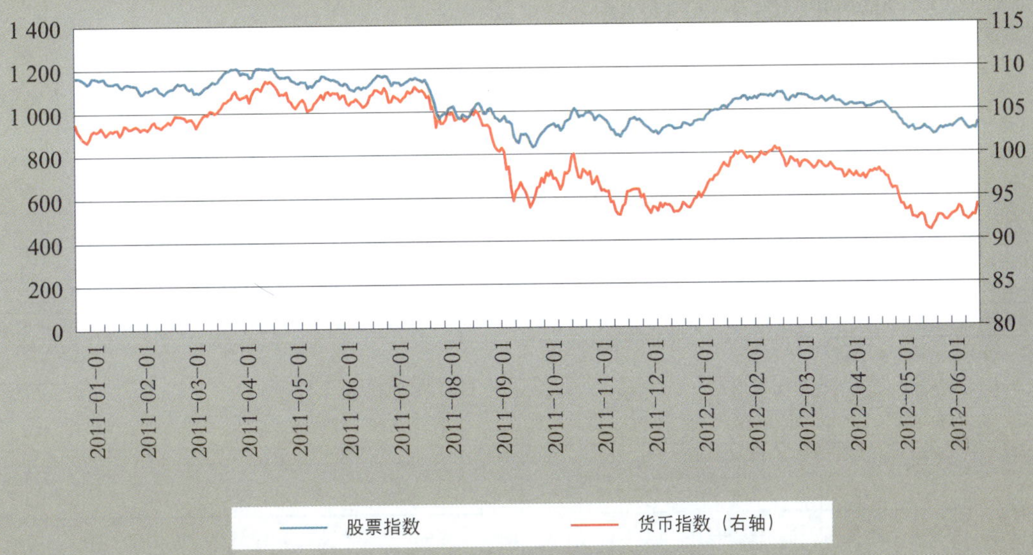

数据来源：彭博资讯、路透。

发展力度加大，央行上半年两次下调存款准备金率共计 1 个百分点，1 次下调存贷款基准利率，加大逆回购操作力度，同时防范和化解金融风险的任务加重。人民币汇率逐步趋近市场认可的合理均衡水平，单边升值的走势和预期明显改变，但另一方面境内主体财务运作方式有所调整，购汇和持汇意愿增强、外汇融资动机减弱。

图 1-4

2008—2012 年上半年我国季度 GDP 和月度 CPI 增长率

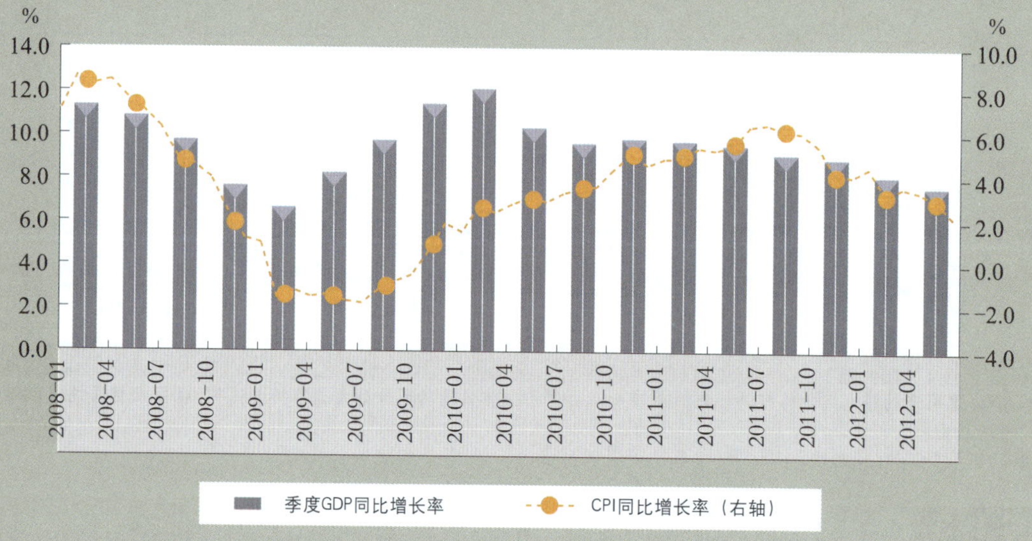

数据来源：国家统计局。

（二）国际收支主要状况

国际收支保持“双顺差”。2012 年上半年，经常项目顺差 772 亿美元，同比下降 12%；资本和金融项目顺差 149 亿美元，下降 92%（见表 1-1）。

表 1-1 2006—2012 年上半年国际收支顺差结构

单位：亿美元

项　目	2006 年	2007 年	2008 年	2009 年	2010 年	2011 年	2012 年上半年
国际收支总差额	2 811	4 474	4 607	4 417	5 247	4 228	921
经常项目差额	2 318	3 532	4 206	2 433	2 378	2 017	772
占国际收支总差额比重（%）	82.5	78.9	91.3	55.1	45.3	47.7	83.9
与 GDP 之比（%）	8.5	10.1	9.3	4.9	4.0	2.8	2.1
资本和金融项目差额	493	942	401	1 985	2 869	2 211	149
占国际收支总差额比重（%）	17.5	21.1	8.7	44.9	54.7	52.3	16.1
与 GDP 之比（%）	1.8	2.7	0.9	4.0	4.8	3.0	0.4

数据来源：国家外汇管理局、国家统计局。

货物贸易顺差有所增长。按国际收支统计口径，2012 年上半年，货物贸易出口

9 577 亿美元，进口 8 449 亿美元，分别较 2011 年同期增长 9% 和 7%；顺差 1 128 亿美元[①]，增长 29%（见图 1–5）。

图 1–5

2001—2012 年上半年经常项目主要子项目的收支状况

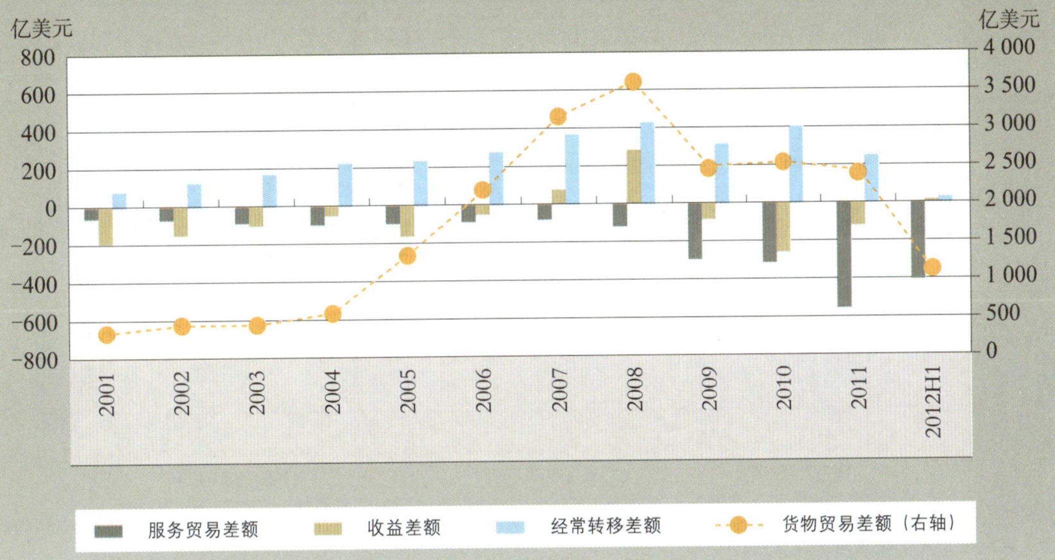

数据来源：国家外汇管理局。

服务贸易逆差进一步扩大。2012 年上半年，服务贸易收入 903 亿美元，与 2011 年同期基本持平；支出 1 305 亿美元，增长 19%；逆差 403 亿美元，增长 104%。上半年，货物与服务贸易顺差合计为 726 亿美元，较上年增长 7%，与 GDP 之比为 2.0%，较 2011 年同期下降 0.2 个百分点（见图 1–6）。

收益项目小幅顺差。2012 年上半年，收益项目收入 902 亿美元，同比增长 22%；支出 885 亿美元，增长 22%；顺差 16 亿美元，下降 11%。其中，投资收益收入和支出分别增长 24% 和 23%，逆差 57 亿美元，增长 7%。若剔除外商投资企业外方未分配利润和已分配未汇出利润的因素，上半年外方实际利润汇出增长 14%，未见明显异常。

直接投资持续较大顺差。按国际收支统计口径，2012 年上半年，直接投资顺差 900 亿美元，同比下降 3%。其中，外国来华直接投资净流入 1 181 亿美元[②]，增长

① 本口径与海关口径的主要差异在于，一是海关统计的到岸价进口额按 5% 减去其中的运输和保险费用后计为国际收支口径的进口，二是国际收支口径还包括货物修理、运输工具在港口购买的货物以及抓获的进出口走私，并分别在进出口中扣除了退货。

② 本口径与商务部公布的数据主要差异在于，国际收支统计中还包括了外商投资企业的未分配利润、已分配未汇出利润、盈余公积、股东贷款、金融机构吸收外资、非居民购买不动产等内容。

6%；我国对外直接投资净流出281亿美元，增长53%（见图1-7）。

图 1-6

1994—2012年上半年货物和服务贸易差额与GDP之比

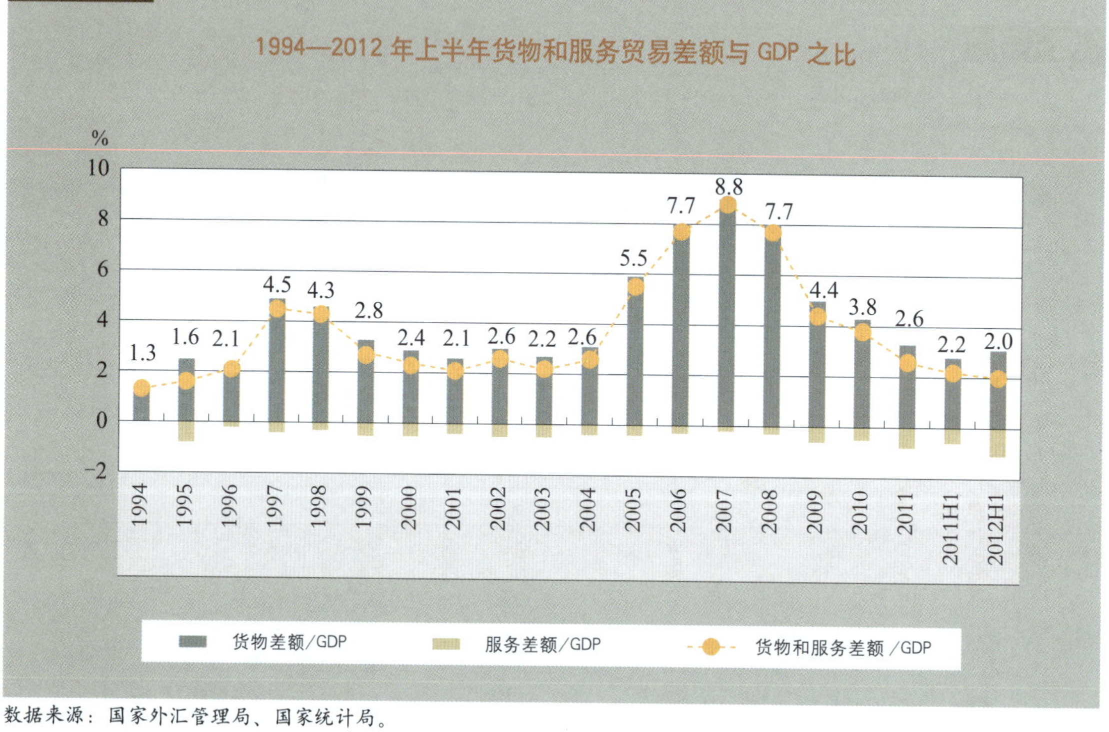

数据来源：国家外汇管理局、国家统计局。

图 1-7

2001—2012年上半年资本和金融项目主要子项目的收支状况

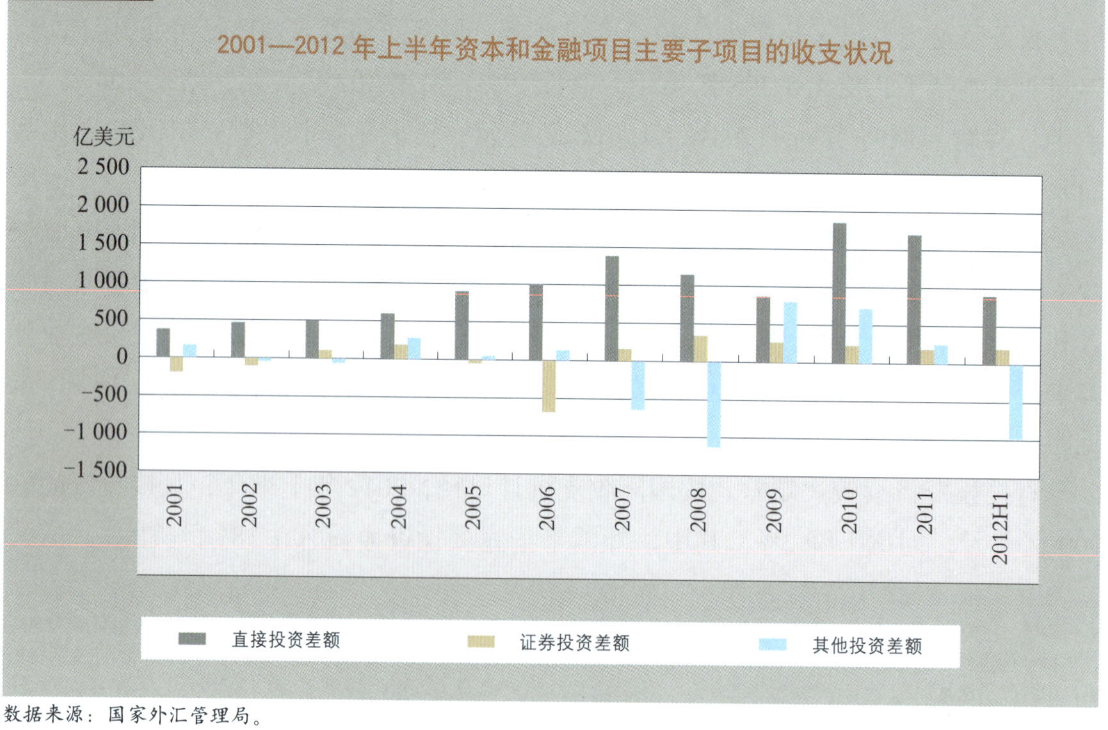

数据来源：国家外汇管理局。

证券投资净流入快速增长。2012年上半年，证券投资项下净流入204亿美元，同比增长1.4倍。其中，我国对外证券投资净回流59亿美元，2011年同期净回流为5亿美元；境外对我国证券投资净流入145亿美元，增长84%。

其他投资呈现较大净流出。2012年上半年，其他投资项下净流出979亿美元，而2011年同期为净流入798亿美元。在人民币汇率双向波动、欧债危机继续发酵等境内外市场因素影响下，我国企业持汇意愿增强，外汇存款增加并形成银行的对外存放款，而企业对外赊账也有所增多，导致其他投资项下对外资产净增加1 623亿美元，同比增长109%。同时，境外对我国企业和银行赊账或存放款增幅放缓，其他投资项下对外负债净增加644亿美元，同比下降59%。

专栏1

如何看待近期外汇存款增长

2012年以来，银行外汇存款增长迅速（见图C1-1），上半年累计增加1 301亿美元，同比多增994亿美元。分析认为，人民币升值预期减弱后，企业调整财务运作是主因，单纯积累外汇资产、看空人民币的现象不明显。

外汇存款增长是企业财务运作调整的结果。过去几年受人民币升值预期的影响，企业的资产本币化、负债外币化倾向明显，积累美元空头是一种合意的经济行为。但随着国际收支、人民币汇率趋向合理均衡水平，特别是在当前本外币利差和汇差条件下，企业开始削减前期积累的美元空头、由过度看空美元回归中性操作。主要表现为：一是以外汇掉期交易的方式买入外汇作为保证金，获得境外银行的人民币代付；二是直接以留存外汇作为外汇保证金，获得境外银行的美元代付。据不完全调查，上半年企业通过境外银行代付、境内银行开立远期信用证和提供对外担保等方式，累计新增跨境贸易融资近500亿美元，同期外汇保证金存款增加583亿美元。外汇保证金存款增量超出跨境贸易融资增量，说明企业逐渐用外汇保证金替代原来的人民币保证金，回补前期未套保的跨境融资美元空头。这种变化是企业适应新环境的正常和积极表现，并非脱离实体经济需要而单纯建立美元多头赌人民币贬值。事实上，当前外汇存款增长也主要集中在企业，2012年上半年个人外汇存款仅增加21亿美元。

外汇存款增长还与银行本外币资金定价有关。过去一段时期国内部分银行外汇存款利率定价偏高、调整滞后，本外币存款的利差明显小于远期外汇市场美元升水幅度，引导一些企业留存外汇收入或通过外汇掉期交易将人民币存款转换为美元存款，同时卖出远期美元，以获得无风险套利，而正常情况下按照利率平价利差与汇差应基本对冲。这种套利活动使银行体系的美元流动性增加，压低美元利率，又推动远期外汇市场美元升水幅度扩大。这表明随着人民币汇率单向预期减弱，国内本外币利率与汇率的定价机制开始回归常态，远期汇率将更多地反映本外币利差而非预期。

上半年，国内外汇贷款增加319亿美元，远低于外汇存款增长，这意味着银行体系只能将吸收的大部分外汇存款转向对外贷款、投资和拆借，反映为银行境外资产增加，在国际收支平衡表中记录为资本和金融项目的流出。由于企业增加的外汇存款并没有离开国内金融体系，只是资金在公司部门与银行部门之间的转移，相当于“藏汇于民”，不代表资本外流。

图 C1–1

2008—2012年上半年金融机构外汇存贷款

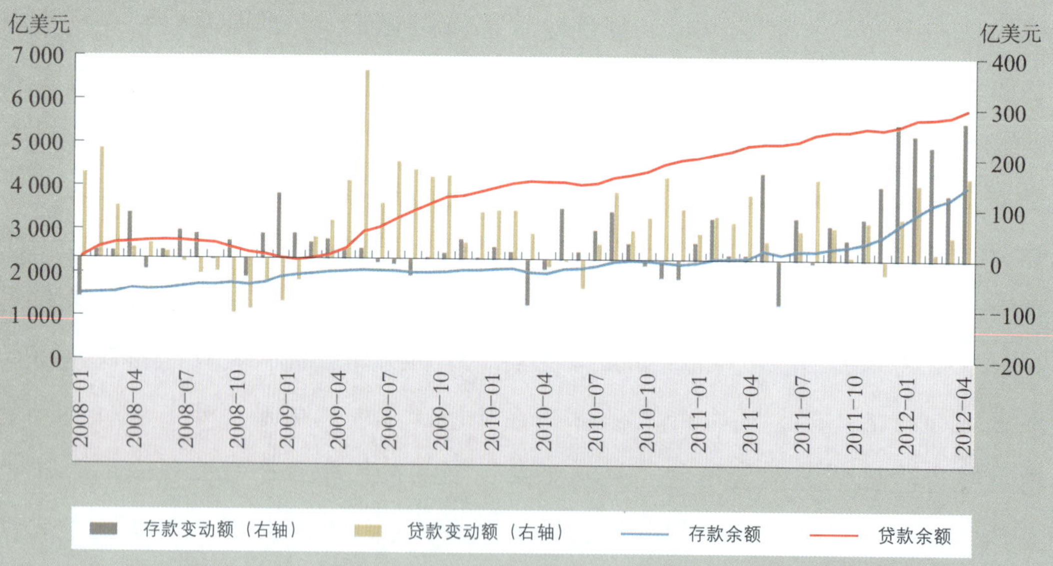

数据来源：中国人民银行。

储备资产增幅放缓。2012年上半年，剔除汇率、价格等非交易价值变动影响（下同），我国新增储备资产629亿美元，同比下降78%。其中，外汇储备资产增加636

亿美元，较2011年同期少增2 174亿美元，截至6月末我国外汇储备余额达32 400亿美元（见图1-8）；我国在国际货币基金组织的储备头寸净减少8亿美元。

图 1-8

2001—2012年上半年外汇储备增加额与外汇储备余额

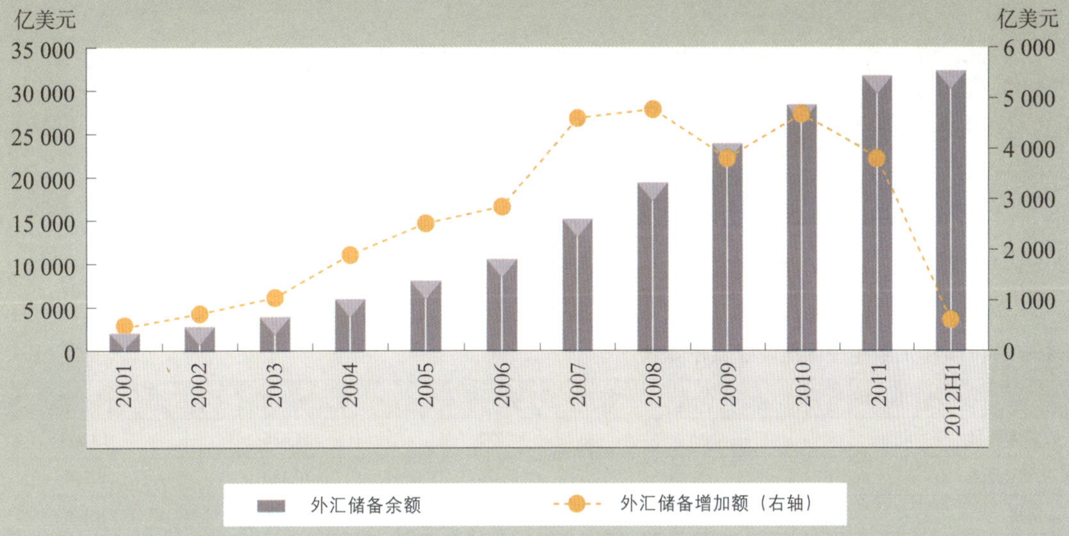

注：图中外汇储备增加额为交易引起的变化，剔除了估值效应的影响。
数据来源：国家外汇管理局。

专栏2

央行外汇占款与外汇储备变动

央行外汇占款余额变动主要包括两个方面：一是中央银行进行外汇买卖时相应投放或吸收的人民币资金变动，二是由于外汇储备经营收益部分结汇而投放的人民币资金变动。

外汇储备变动主要有两个口径：一是国际收支平衡表的外汇储备资产变动，包括中央银行通过外汇买卖形成的储备变化，以及当期储备经营收益。二是外汇储备余额变动，除国际收支口径的外汇储备资产变动外，还包括价格、汇率等非交易因素引起的储备价值变动。

因此，从概念口径上看，外汇储备余额变动大于国际收支口径的外汇储备资产变动大于央行外汇占款余额变动（见图C2-1）。

图 C2-1

央行外汇占款与外汇储备变动的关系图

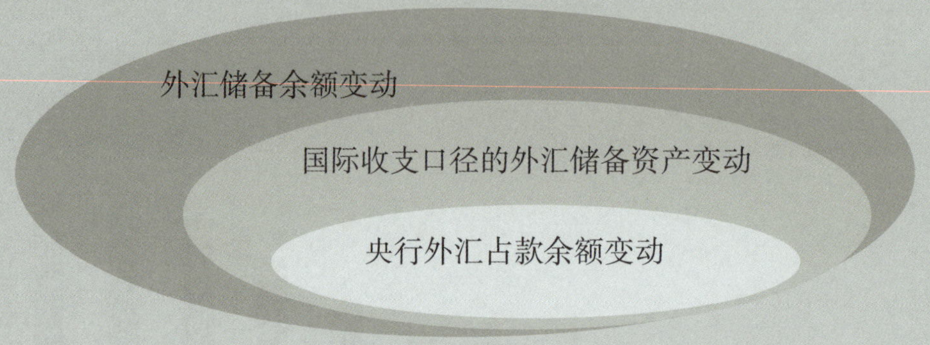

表 1-2　2012 年上半年中国国际收支平衡表[①]

单位：亿美元

项　目	差　额	贷　方	借　方
一、经常项目	**772**	**11 636**	**10 863**
A. 货物和服务	**726**	**10 480**	**9 754**
a. 货物	**1 128**	**9 577**	**8 449**
b. 服务	**−403**	**903**	**1 305**
1. 运输	−229	184	414
2. 旅游	−218	238	456
3. 通讯服务	3	9	6
4. 建筑服务	46	61	15
5. 保险服务	−84	17	100
6. 金融服务	−1	4	5
7. 计算机和信息服务	53	69	16
8. 专有权利使用费和特许费	−85	4	89
9. 咨询	66	157	91
10. 广告、宣传	9	23	14
11. 电影、音像	−2	1	2
12. 其他商业服务	40	132	92
13. 别处未提及的政府服务	−1	4	5
B. 收益	**16**	**902**	**885**
1. 职工报酬	73	82	9
2. 投资收益	−57	820	876
C. 经常转移	**31**	**255**	**224**
1. 各级政府	−15	4	19

① 我国国际收支平衡表按国际货币基金组织《国际收支手册》第五版规定的各项原则编制，采用复式记账原则记录所有发生在我国居民（不包括港、澳、台地区）与非居民之间的经济交易。本表计数采用四舍五入原则。

续表

项　目	差　额	贷　方	借　方
2. 其他部门	46	250	205
二、资本和金融项目	**149**	**6 527**	**6 378**
A. 资本项目	**24**	**25**	**1**
B. 金融项目	**125**	**6 501**	**6 377**
1. 直接投资	**900**	**1 414**	**514**
1.1 我国在外直接投资	−281	100	380
1.2 外国在华直接投资	1 181	1 314	133
2. 证券投资	**204**	**310**	**106**
2.1 资产	59	143	85
2.1.1 股本证券	22	50	28
2.1.2 债务证券	36	93	57
2.1.2.1（中）长期债券	52	87	35
2.1.2.2 货币市场工具	−16	6	22
2.2 负债	145	166	21
2.2.1 股本证券	53	74	21
2.2.2 债务证券	92	92	0
2.2.2.1（中）长期债券	71	71	0
2.2.2.2 货币市场工具	21	21	0
3. 其他投资	**−979**	**4 778**	**5 757**
3.1 资产	−1 623	265	1 887
3.1.1 贸易信贷	−332	4	336
长期	−7	0	7
短期	−326	4	330
3.1.2 贷款	−431	7	438
长期	−183	0	183
短期	−248	7	255
3.1.3 货币和存款	−967	146	1 113
3.1.4 其他资产	108	108	0
长期	0	0	0
短期	108	108	0
3.2 负债	644	4 513	3 870
3.2.1 贸易信贷	409	409	0
长期	7	7	0
短期	402	402	0
3.2.2 贷款	379	3 394	3 015
长期	87	245	158
短期	292	3 149	2 857
3.2.3 货币和存款	−183	658	841
3.2.4 其他负债	39	53	14
长期	43	43	0
短期	−4	10	14

续表

项　目	差　额	贷　方	借　方
三、储备资产	**-629**	**121**	**750**
1. 货币黄金	0	0	0
2. 特别提款权	-1	1	2
3. 在基金组织的储备头寸	8	8	0
4. 外汇	-636	0	636
5. 其他债权	0	0	0
四、净误差与遗漏	**-292**	**0**	**292**

数据来源：国家外汇管理局。

（三）国际收支运行评价

涉外经济活动平稳增长。2012 年上半年，国际收支交易总规模为 3.54 万亿美元，较上年同期增长 10%；与同期 GDP 之比为 98%，较 2011 年同期略降 5 个百分点（见图 1-9）。其中，国际收支口径的货物和服务贸易总规模同比增长 8%，跨国直接投资（包括外国来华直接投资和我国对外直接投资）交易总规模增长 14%。

图 1-9

1990—2012 年上半年国际收支交易规模及其与 GDP 之比

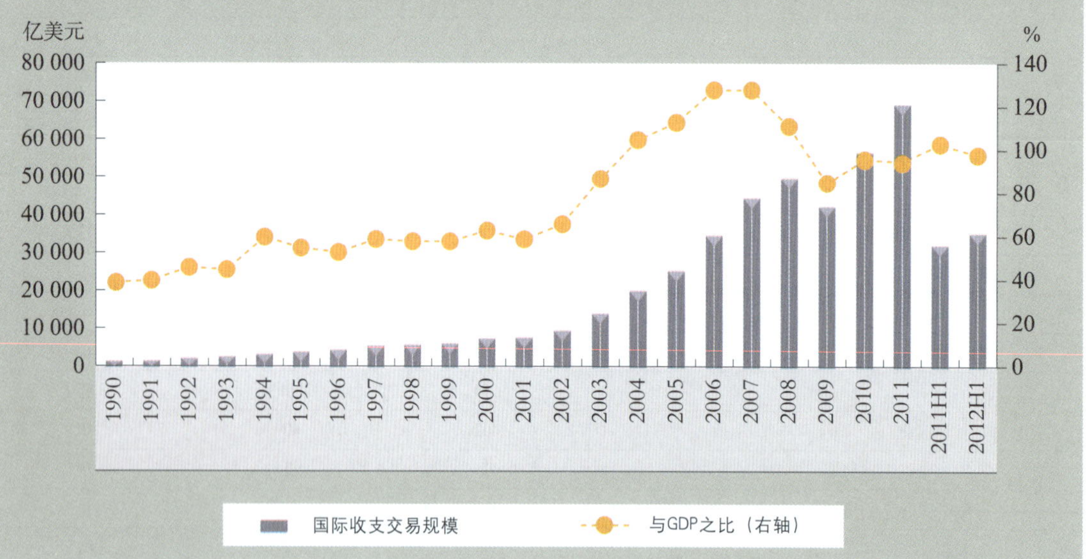

数据来源：国家外汇管理局、国家统计局。

国际收支趋向更加平衡。2012 年上半年，国际收支总顺差 921 亿美元，回落至 2005 年同期的顺差水平，同比下降 66%。经常项目顺差与 GDP 之比为 2.1%，较 2011 年同期下降 0.7 个百分点。储备资产增幅明显放缓，与 GDP 之比为 1.7%，同比下降 7.3 个百分点（见图 1-10）。

图 1-10

1990—2012 年上半年经常项目差额和储备资产增加额与 GDP 之比

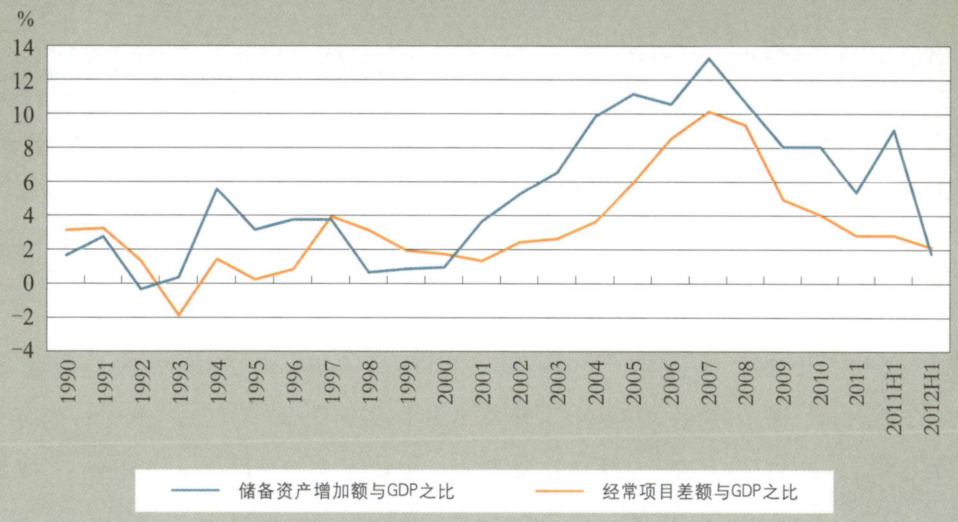

数据来源：国家外汇管理局、国家统计局。

跨境资本流动呈现双向变化。2012 年第一季度，随着国际市场环境转暖，国际资本回流我国，资本和金融项目由 2011 年第四季度的逆差 290 亿美元转为顺差 561 亿美元；第二季度，在实体经济增速趋缓、欧债危机继续发酵、市场避险情绪上升等因素作用下再现净流出 412 亿美元。

专栏 3

资本项目逆差≠外资集中撤离

2012 年上半年我国资本和金融项目顺差 149 亿美元，其中第二季度为逆差 412 亿美元。这主要是受国内外因素的共同影响，但这不等于外资大规模集中撤离。从理论上讲，经常项目顺差大于外汇储备增加额，意味着我国境内机构和个人资本呈现净输出（即国际收支平衡表中资本项目逆差）、对外净资产增多。尤其是 2012 年 4 月进一步扩大人民币汇率浮动区间，大幅减少央行外汇干预以后，更加强化了这种经常项目顺差、资本项目逆差的国际收支自主平衡格局。从国际收支统计细项数据看，也印证了资本项目逆差主要是外汇资产持有从央行转向境内机构和个人，藏汇于民的过程，外资主动撤离的迹象尚不明显。

从直接投资来看，虽然第二季度直接投资顺差411亿美元（见图C3-1），同比下降14%。但这并不是外商撤资造成的，第二季度，外国来华直接投资撤资75亿美元，同比增长6%，低于同期资本和金融项目流出的平均增速（25%），也低于2001年以来外商直接投资撤资的季度平均增速（38%）。直接投资顺差下降的主要原因是我国企业趁海外资产走低，积极“走出去”，对外直接投资增长17%，达到195亿美元。

从证券投资来看，第二季度证券投资仍为顺差111亿美元，较上季度增长20%。主要来源：一是欧债危机反复后我国对外证券投资净回流25亿美元，二是对境外人民币持有者开放银行间货币市场后非居民人民币债券投资流入30多亿美元，三是境内企业海外筹资及QFII项下资金净流入合计35亿美元。

从其他投资来看，第二季度逆差较大，主要是境内银行对外贷款和存款净流出较多，达890亿美元，占其他投资资产项下净流出额的73%。同期，其他投资的负债项下仍表现为资金净流入，达270亿美元，包括贸易信贷、贷款等资金，说明我国境内机构在海外市场仍具有一定的融资能力。

图C3-1

2007—2012年上半年资本和金融项目主要子项目的季度收支状况

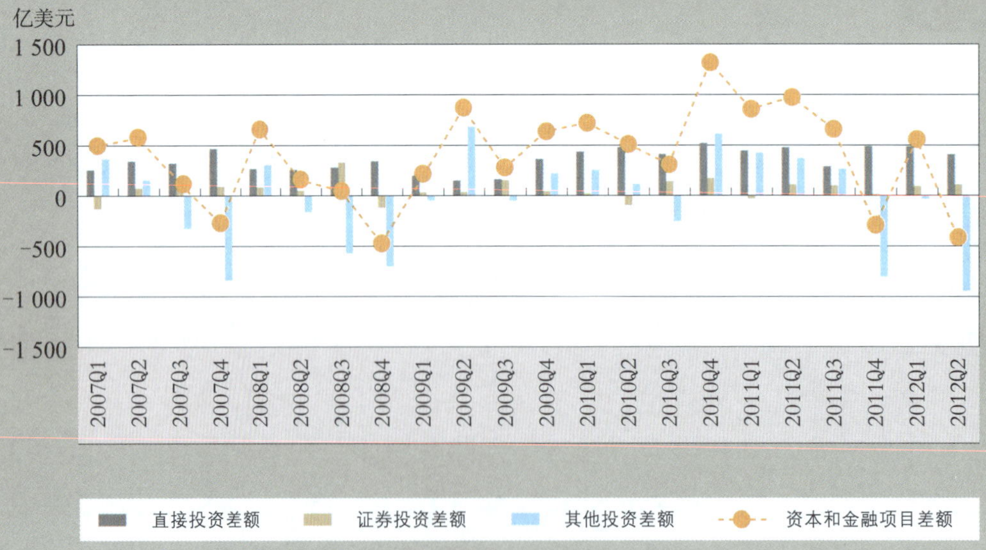

数据来源：国家外汇管理局。

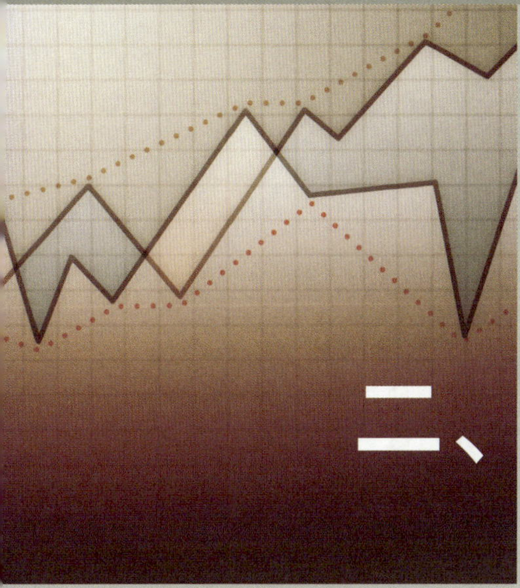

二、国际收支主要项目分析

（一）货物贸易

据海关统计，2012 年上半年我国货物贸易呈现以下特点：

对外贸易增速放缓，外贸依存度较上年同期有所回落。上半年，进出口总额同比增长 8%，增速较上年同期回落 18 个百分点。出口、进口及进出口总额与同期 GDP 之比分别为 26.5%、24.6% 和 51.1%，较上年同期分别回落 1.3 个、1.8 个和 3.1 个百分点（见图 2–1），显示我国经济增长的内生性进一步增强。

图 2–1

2000—2012 年上半年进口、出口与同期 GDP 之比

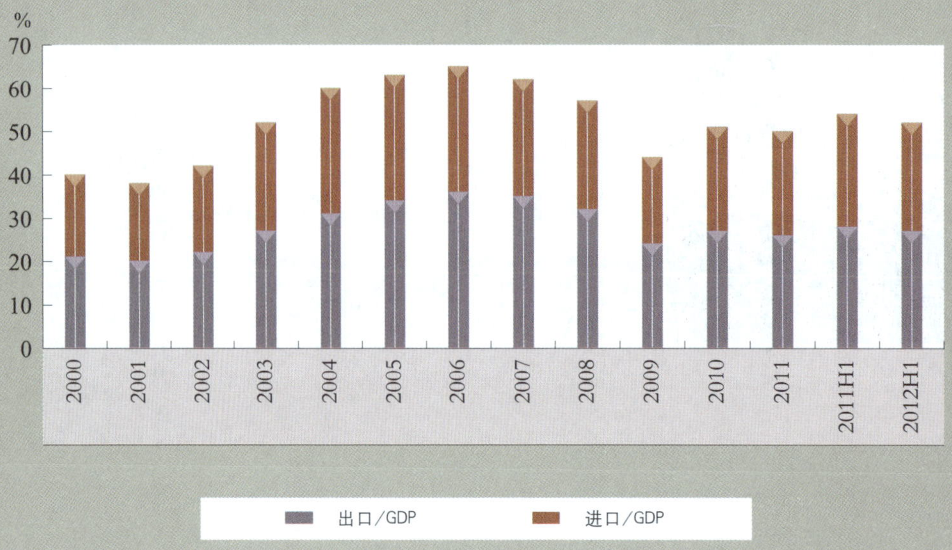

数据来源：海关总署、国家统计局。

出口增速快于进口，外贸顺差有所反弹。上半年，出口同比增长 9%，进口增长 7%，进出口顺差 689 亿美元，增长 56%；顺差与同期 GDP 之比为 1.9%，较上年同期提高 0.5 个百分点（见图 2–2）。进口增长较慢，一是由于进口价格增幅明显回落，降低了我国的进口成本。随着国际大宗商品价格下行，上半年，我国进口价格月均同比微增 1.7%，较 2011 年同期增幅回落 13.1 个百分点，进口数量指数月均同比增长 6.4%，增幅回落 5.1 个百分点（见图 2–3）。二是由于加工贸易出口增长低迷，影响了与加工再出口相关的进口需求。上半年，我国加工贸易出口增长 6.4%，低于一般贸易出口增速近 4 个百分点，导致同期加工贸易进口增长 0.7%，较一般贸易进口增速低 7 个百分点（见图 2–4）。

图 2-2

2000—2012 年上半年进出口差额及其与 GDP 之比

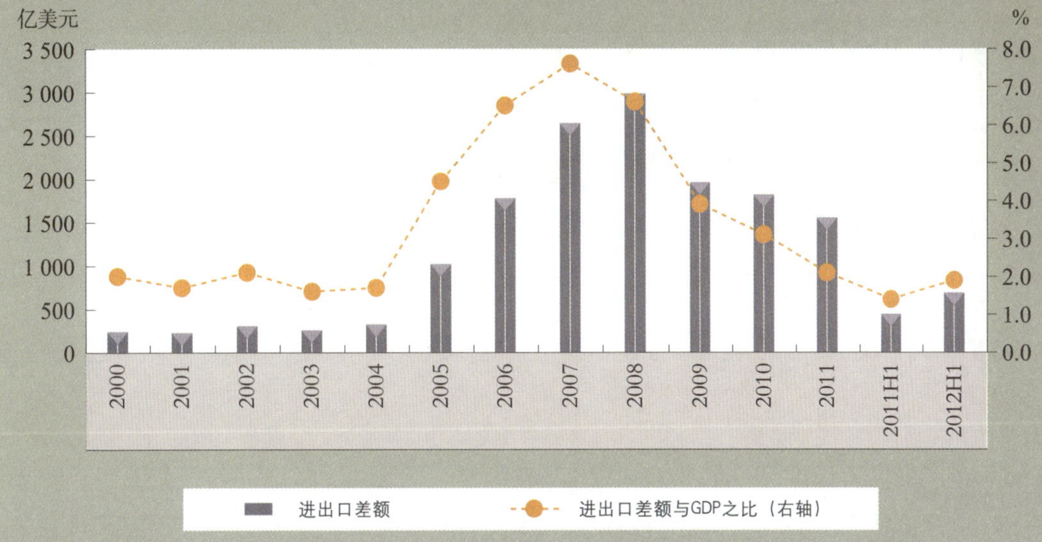

数据来源：海关总署、国家统计局。

图 2-3

2010 年 1 月至 2012 年 6 月进出口数量和价格变动

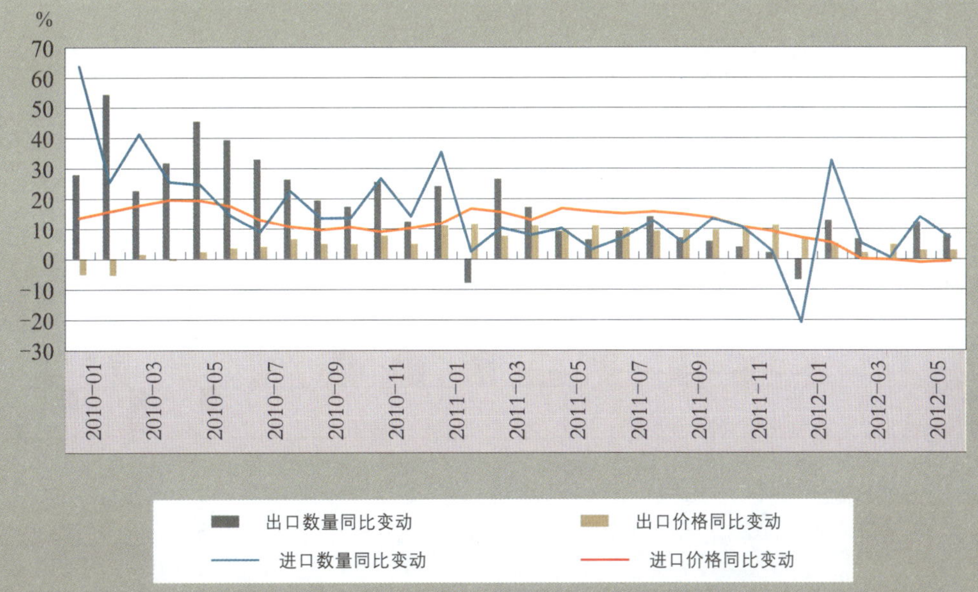

数据来源：海关总署。

图 2-4

2000—2012 年上半年不同贸易方式进出口增速

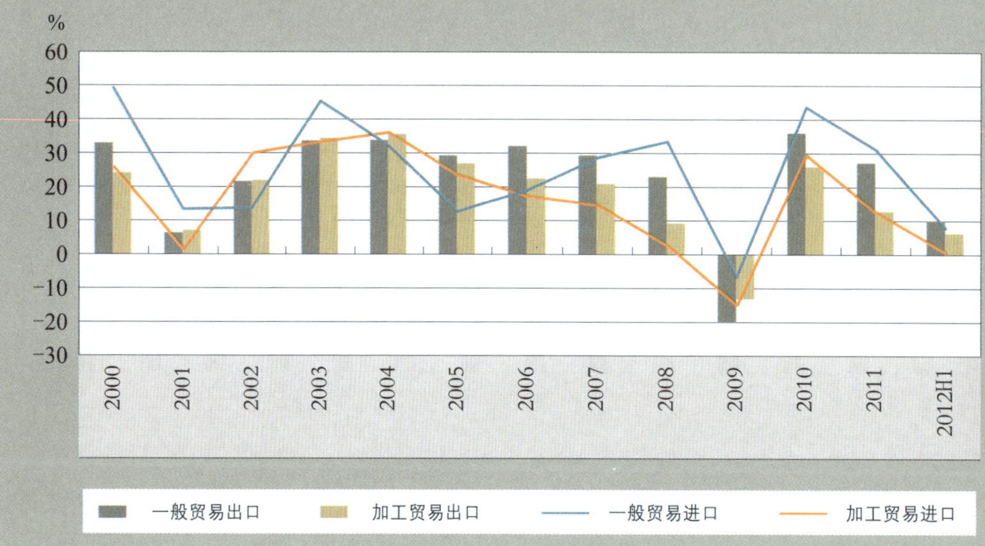

数据来源：海关总署。

加工贸易顺差扩大，一般贸易逆差收窄。2012 年上半年，我国加工贸易顺差 1 874 亿美元，同比增长 14%。其中，外商投资企业加工贸易顺差 1 631 亿美元，同比增长 15%，占加工贸易总顺差的 87%，较上年同期提高 1 个百分点。同期，

图 2-5

2000—2012 年上半年货物贸易差额主要构成

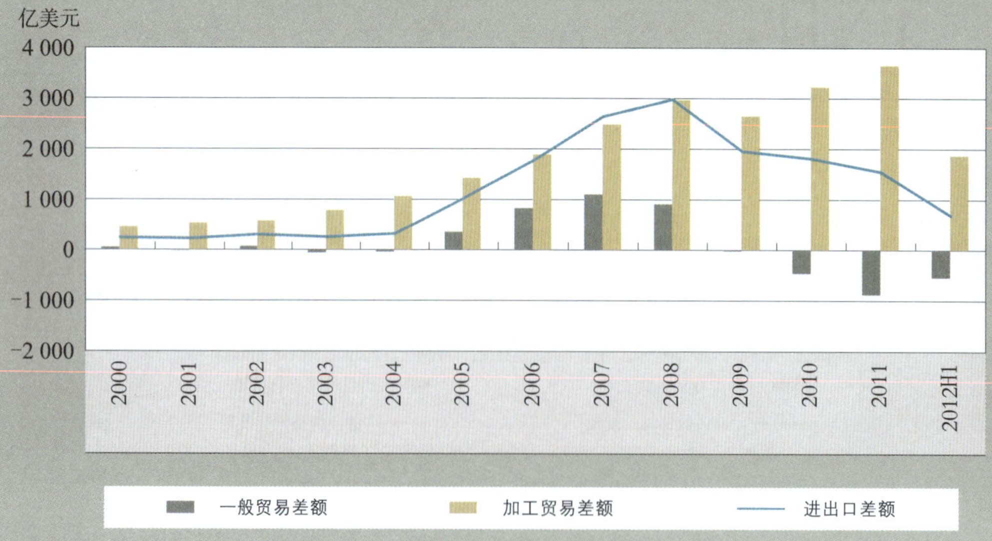

数据来源：海关总署。

我国一般贸易逆差为539亿美元（见图2-5），同比减少7%，主要是由于以私营性质为主的其他企业一般贸易出口增长较快。

外贸多元化进一步推进，与新兴经济体的贸易增速快于发达经济体。上半年，我国与南非、俄罗斯、巴西和东盟的双边贸易额增长较快（见图2-6），分别较总体增速高29个、14个、4个和2个百分点，所占比重合计较上年同期提高0.8个百分点。但与欧盟贸易额仅增长0.7%，与日本的贸易额同比下降0.2%，所占比重合计较上年同期下降1.8个百分点。我国与美国贸易额同比增长12%，比重略有增加。

图2-6

与主要贸易伙伴进出口增速及进出口额占比变动情况

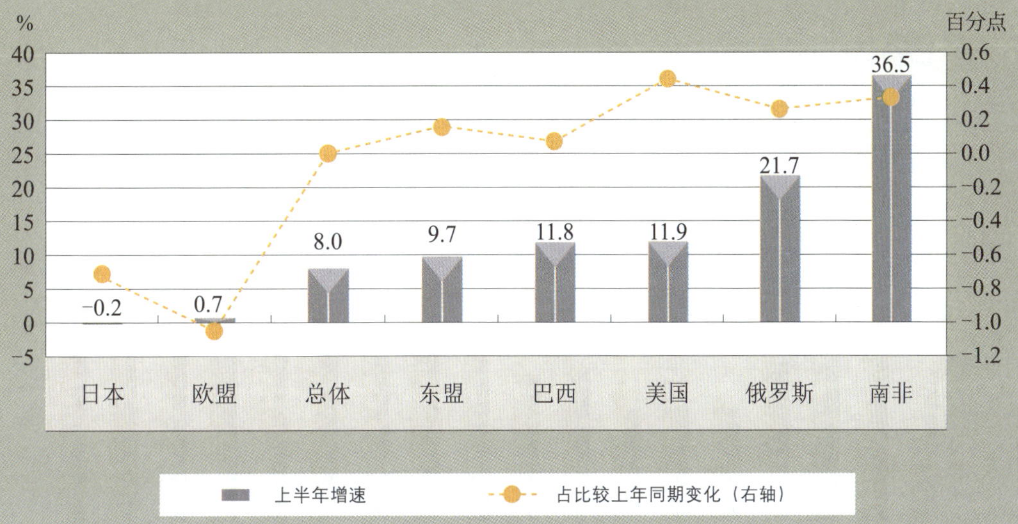

数据来源：海关总署。

专栏4

当前我国出口收汇情况分析

我国出口形势对出口收汇的影响较大。据海关统计，2012年上半年出口同比增长9%，增速明显低于去年同期24%的增长水平。受此影响，出口收汇增长也较低迷，据国际收支申报统计，上半年出口收汇（货物贸易跨境收入）同比增长8%，增速远低于去年同期29%的增长水平。

上半年我国出口收汇总体较稳定，但下滑态势值得关注。一般情况下，出口货物流与跨境收入资金流之间存在差异，影响因素一是出口预收和延收问题，可以在一定程度上反映出口货款的回收速度及风险，此外也与出口企业的收汇意愿有关；二是出口不需收汇的特殊情况、季节性波动和统计口径等，但这些因素不随外贸环境的改变而变化，可以认为相对稳定。2012年上半年，我国出口收汇率（货物贸易跨境收入/出口）为91%，仍保持在较高水平，较2011年上半年略降1个百分点。但第二季度出口收汇率为85%，相对第一季度下滑较大，并且也低于2011年同期5个百分点（见图C4-1）。这一方面说明我国出口收汇受到2011年底以来境外流动性趋紧、交易对手资金状况不佳等因素影响，出现一定的收汇风险；另一方面也反映了在人民币汇率双向波动的情况下，境内企业出口后尽快尽早收结汇的意愿降低。

图 C4-1

2010年第一季度至2012年第二季度出口及其跨境收入情况

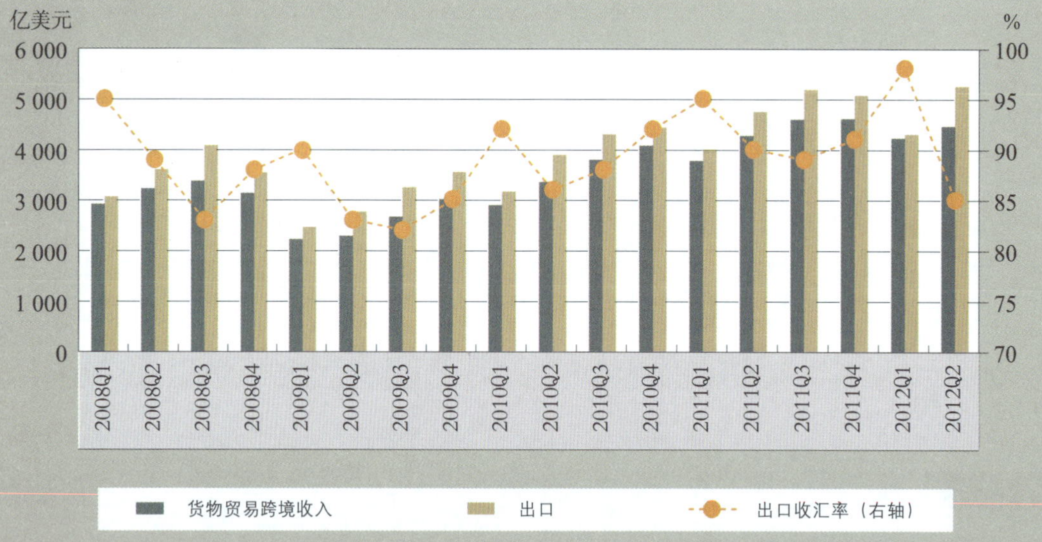

数据来源：国家外汇管理局、海关总署。

未来仍需高度关注出口收汇风险。受外部经济复苏放缓、欧债危机继续发酵、国际金融市场不稳定因素较多等影响，我国企业在特定阶段或特定地区的出口收汇不确定性依然较大。下一阶段，外汇管理部门将继续支持国家稳定外贸增长的政策，稳步推进货物贸易外汇管理改革，进一步将促进贸易便利的政策措施落到实处，切实增强企业出口竞争力，并防范出口收汇风险。

（二）服务贸易

服务贸易规模保持较快增长。按国际收支统计口径，2012 年上半年服务贸易总额为 2 208 亿美元，同比增长 10%，增速较货物贸易高 2 个百分点。服务贸易总额相当于货物贸易总额的 12%，该比例与上年同期持平（见图 2-7）。

图 2-7

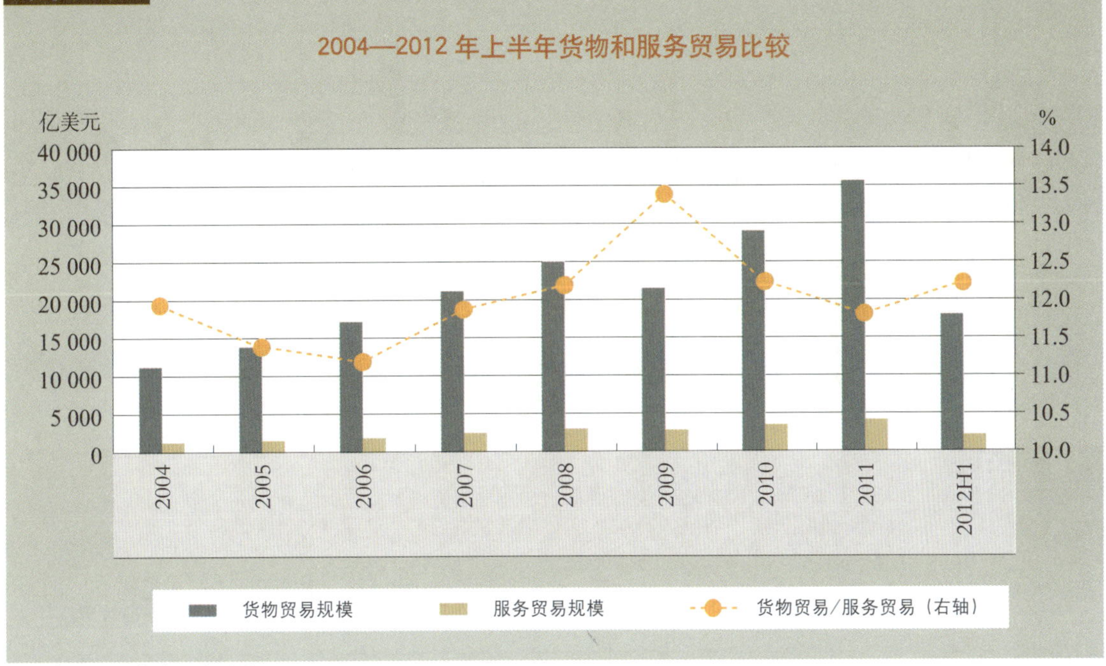

数据来源：国家外汇管理局。

运输和旅游项目较大逆差是服务贸易逆差大幅上升的主要原因。2012 年上半年，服务贸易逆差 403 亿美元，较上年同期增长一倍。其中，运输逆差 229 亿美元，旅游逆差 218 亿美元，分别较上年同期增长 10% 和 1.1 倍。运输项目长期保持较大逆差主要是由于我国外贸进出口总量持续增加，境内企业对国际货物运输的需求上升，带动运输服务支出较快增长。旅游方面，上半年，外籍人员入境旅游 1 346 万人次，同比增长 5%，带动住宿、餐饮购物等旅游收入略有增长；内地居民出境 3 856 万人次，增长 20%，带动境外观光、购物、留学等旅游支出大幅增加。从分国别和地区的情况看，我国对美国、澳大利亚和香港地区均呈现较大规模的旅游逆差（见图 2-8），主要是由于上述三地的留学费用快速增长所致。

服务贸易伙伴国家和地区集中度高。主要服务贸易伙伴集中在邻近地区和欧美发达国家，服务贸易收支前十名伙伴国家和地区占服务贸易总额的 73%（见图 2-9）。其中，对香港地区顺差 180 亿美元，对其他主要伙伴国家和地区均呈现逆差，逆差较大的国家包括澳大利亚、美国和韩国，分别为 59 亿、56 亿和 52 亿美元。

图 2-8

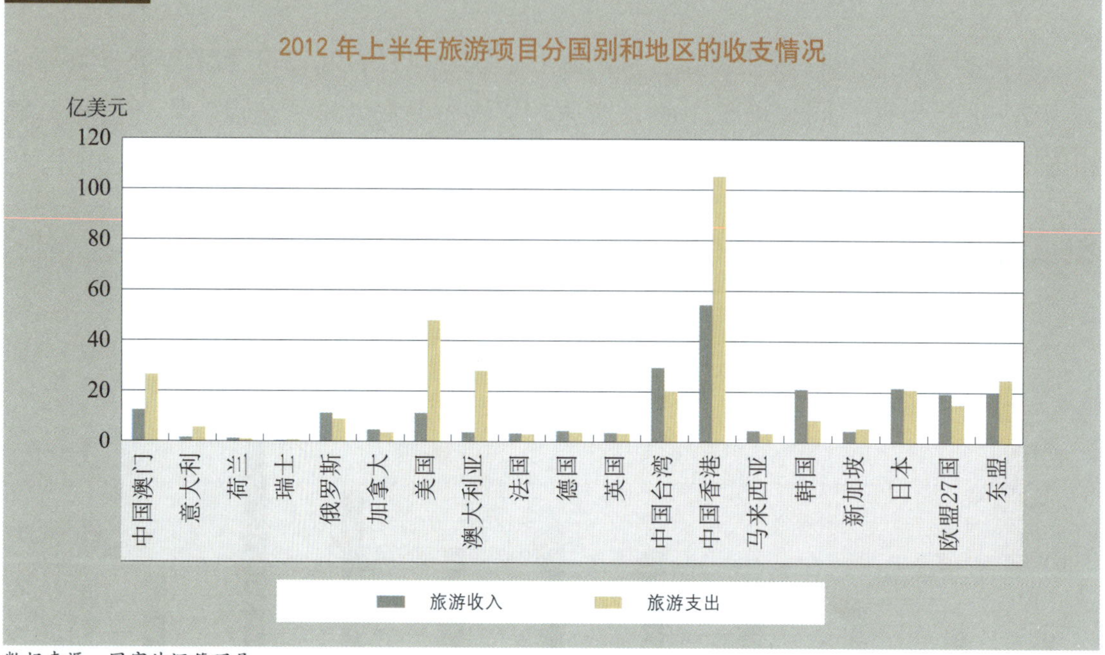

数据来源：国家外汇管理局。

图 2-9

数据来源：国家外汇管理局。

（三）直接投资

直接投资净流入依然是我国国际收支顺差的主要来源。2012 年上半年，直接投资顺差 900 亿美元，同比下降 3%（见图 2-10）。但直接投资净流入在国际收支总顺差中的占比达98%，较上年同期上升64个百分点。这一方面显示直接投资对于我国国际收支状况的稳定作用，另一方面也说明在外部经济环境多变的情况下，我国经济发展稳定、吸引力强，作为世界主要直接投资流入国的地位依然稳固。

图 2-10

2000—2012 年上半年直接投资顺差情况

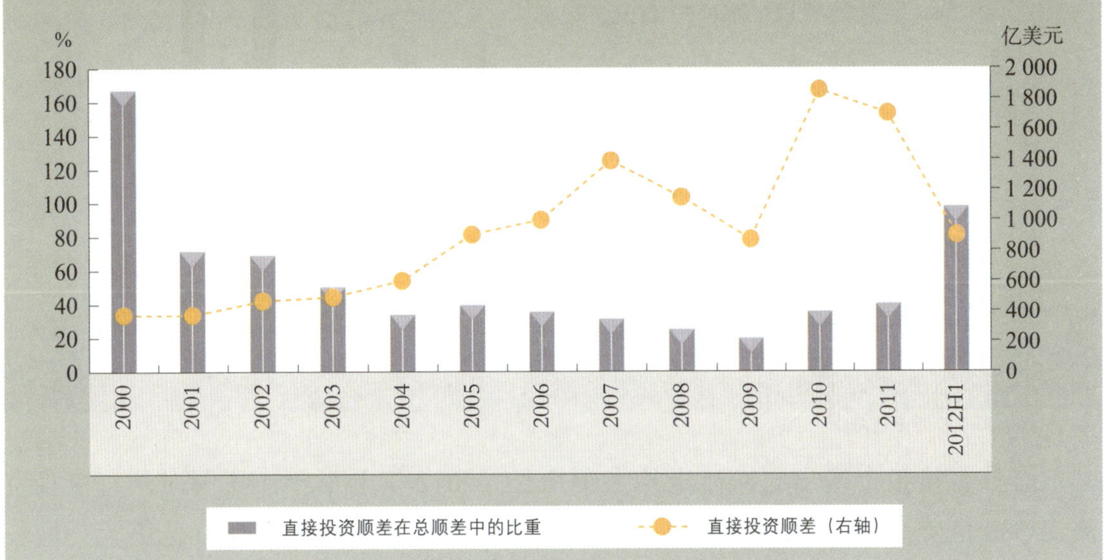

数据来源：国家外汇管理局。

外国来华直接投资流入及净流入均小幅增长。2012年上半年，外国来华直接投资流入1 314亿美元，较上年同期增长7%；外国来华直接投资流出133亿美元，增长15%，主要是由于外商投资企业向境外股东加速偿还贷款，上半年此项增幅达50%，来华直接投资撤资清算流出金额较上年同期下降8%。由于来华直接投资流入规模远高于流出，上半年外国来华直接投资净流入1 181亿美元，增加70亿美元，增长6%，延续了自2009年上半年以来的增长趋势（见图2-11），但增幅有所下降。

外国来华直接投资的结构进一步优化。来自世界主要发达国家的投资持续稳定增长，2012年上半年，法国、德国、日本及美国对我国非银行部门的直接投资金额较上年同期分别增长了110%、96%、29%和20%。来自世界主要离岸中心的直接投资有所下降，开曼群岛、英属维尔京群岛及中国香港对我国内地非银行部门的直接投资金额较上年同期分别下降了37%、35%和15%。从吸收外国来华直接投资的行业分布看，制造业、房地产业、租赁和商务服务业、批发零售业和采矿业仍然是吸收外国来华直接投资的主要行业。与上年同期相比，教育和卫生行业吸收来华直接投资的增长较快，增幅分别为200%与110%；房地产业吸收来华直接投资额下降比较明显，降幅达25%，从侧面反映出国家房地产市场调控的积极效果。

图 2-11

2000—2012 年上半年外国来华直接投资情况

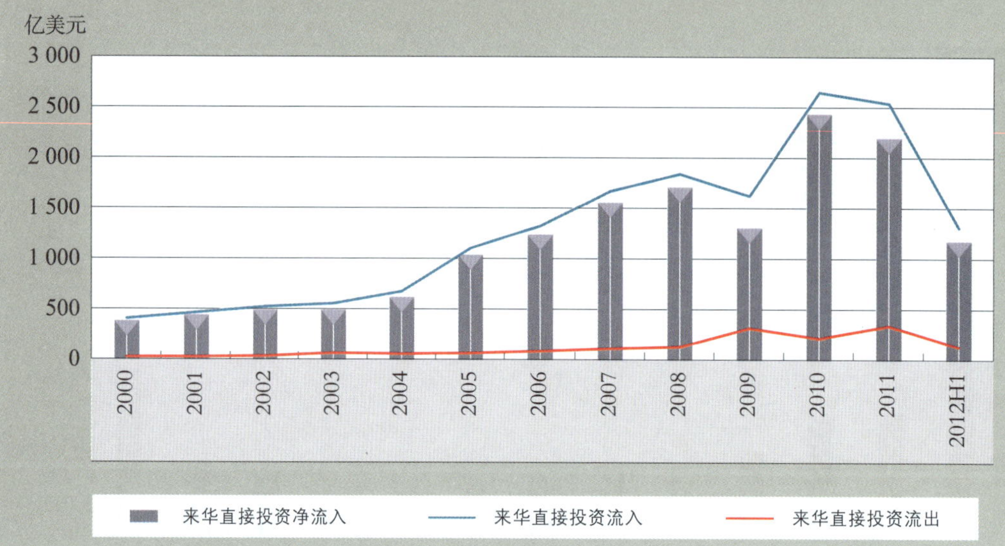

数据来源：国家外汇管理局。

对外直接投资流出与净流出均大幅增长。2012 年上半年，我国对外直接投资流出 380 亿美元，同比增长 45%；我国对外直接投资撤资流入 100 亿美元，增长 25%。由于对外直接投资流出的增幅高于流入，我国对外直接投资净流出 281 亿美元，增长 53%（见图 2-12）。

图 2-12

2000—2012 年上半年我国对外直接投资情况

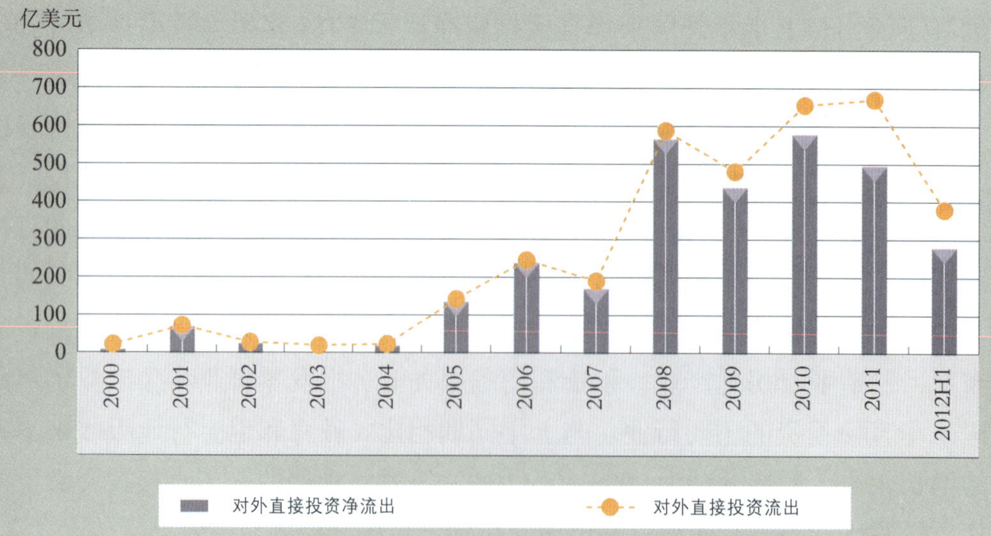

数据来源：国家外汇管理局。

（四）证券投资

证券投资继续保持顺差。2012 年上半年，我国证券投资项下净流入 204 亿美元，较上年同期增长 1.4 倍。其中，我国对外证券投资净流入 59 亿美元，较上年同期大幅增长 9.9 倍；境外对我国证券投资净流入 145 亿美元，较上年同期上升 84%（见图 2-13）。

我国对外证券投资回撤明显。2012 年上半年，世界经济缓慢复苏，欧洲主权债务危机深化，国际金融市场动荡加剧，我国对外证券投资更趋谨慎，新增投资流出 85 亿美元，同比下降 23%，减持回流 143 亿美元，同比上升 24%。其中，对外股本证券投资流出入双降，总体呈净回流 22 亿美元；对外债务证券撤资回流规模上升 1 倍，净回流 36 亿美元，而上年同期为净流出 2 亿美元。2012 年上半年，我国合格境内机构投资者（QDII）对外证券投资大幅波动，第一季度回流 5 亿美元，第二季度汇出 6 亿美元，总体净增对外投资 1 亿美元。

图 2-13

2000—2012 年上半年证券投资差额情况

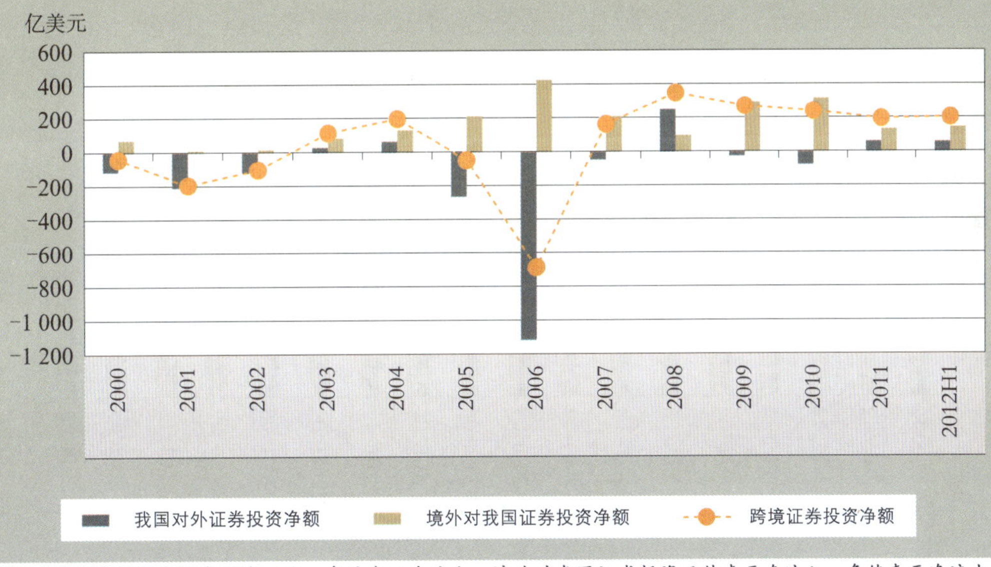

注：我国对外证券投资正值表示净回流，负值表示净流出；境外对我国证券投资正值表示净流入，负值表示净流出。
数据来源：国家外汇管理局。

境外对我国证券投资活跃。2012 年上半年，境外对我国证券投资流入 166 亿美元，流出 21 亿美元，同比分别上升 86% 和 95%。从结构上看，因我国物价水平涨幅持续回落，降息预期强烈，境外更青睐对我国债务证券投资。2012 年上半年，境外人民币清算行等三类机构运用人民币投资境内银行间债券市场踊跃，加之财政部和境内机构在香港离岸市场发行人民币债券，境外对我国债券投资净流入 92 亿美元，上年同期为微量净流出。股票投资方面，受境内企业盈利预期下降和海外资本市场低迷等因素影响，境外对我国股本证券投资流入74亿美元，流出21亿美元，分别下降17%和上升96%，净流入53亿美元，同比下降33%。其中，境内企业海外上市筹资39亿美元，同比下降35%；合格境外机构投资者（QFII）对我国证券投资稳中趋升，第一季度流出入基本平衡，第二季度净流入大幅增至15亿美元，总体净增16亿美元。

（五）贸易信贷

贸易信贷[①]资产负债规模持续增长。2012年6月末，贸易信贷资产余额3 101亿美元，较上年末增加332亿美元，增长12%；贸易信贷负债余额2 901亿美元，较上年末增加409亿美元，增长16%；净资产为200亿美元，较上年末减少77亿美元，下降28%。截至6月末，贸易信贷资产和负债占过去12个月海关进出口总额的比重分别为8.2%和7.7%，较上年末比重分别增加0.6个和0.8个百分点（见图2–14）。

图 2–14

2005年末至2012年6月末贸易信贷资产负债余额

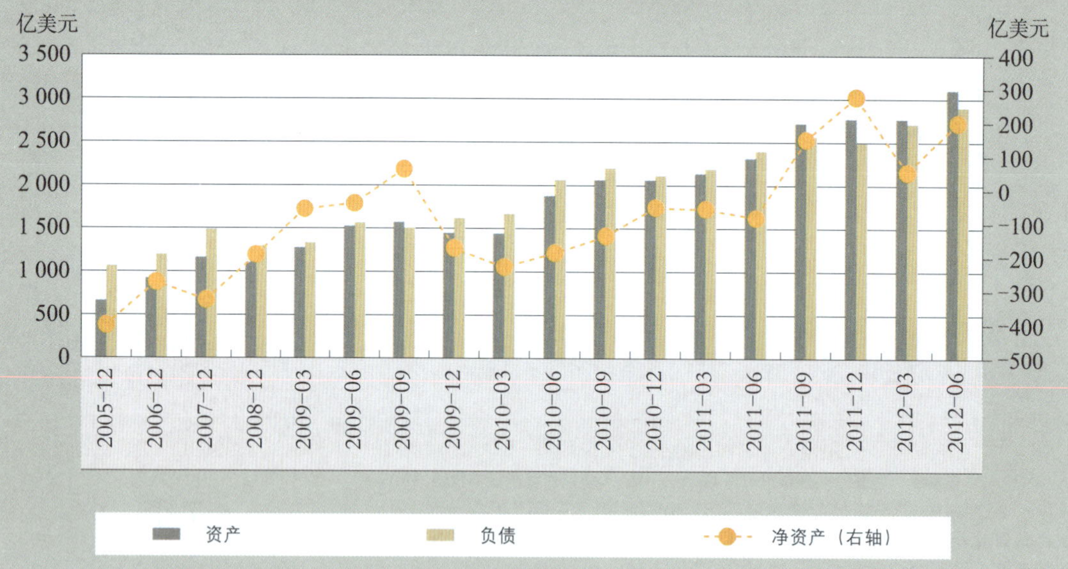

数据来源：国家外汇管理局。

① 贸易信贷指中国境内外企业因贸易往来而相互赊账，形成的应收/预付账款（资产方）和预收/延付账款（负债方），它反映了贸易双方占用对方资金的情况。银行提供的贸易融资和融资性担保不在此列。贸易信贷的资产方和负债方是国际收支平衡表中“资本和金融项目”下“其他投资”项下的重要子项目。其中，贸易信贷的负债方也是我国外债统计的一个重要数据源，与登记外债构成我国外债余额统计。

贸易信贷在波动中呈现净流入。2012 年上半年，我国贸易信贷项下为净流入 77 亿美元。其中，第一季度，因为负债增加、资产减少，贸易信贷净资产显示为大幅下降（即净流入）223 亿美元；第二季度，由于资产增加、负债减少，贸易信贷净资产转为大幅上升（即净流出）147 亿美元。

贸易信贷出口与进口双方向增长。2012 年 6 月末，出口应收款（即少收汇）2 566 亿美元，较上年末增长 17%；出口预收款（即多收汇）589 亿美元，较上年末增长 2%；出口少收汇多于出口多收汇 1 977 亿美元。进口预付款（即多付汇）536 亿美元，较上年末下降 7%；进口应付款（即少付汇）2 312 亿美元，较上年末增长 21%；进口少付汇多于多付汇 1 776 亿美元。

贸易信贷短期化趋势更为明显。2012 年 6 月末，样本企业短期（一年以下）贸易信贷资产占其全部资产的比重为 95%，较上年末增长 5 个百分点；样本企业短期贸易信贷负债占其全部负债的比重为 94%，较上年末增长 1 个百分点。

外商投资企业较内资企业的贸易信贷更为活跃。截至 2012 年 6 月末，样本外商投资企业贸易信贷资产占全部资产的比重为 57%，样本外商投资企业贸易信贷负债占全部负债的比重为 53%。外商投资企业更多利用应收 / 应付进行资金安排，外资应收应付金额占应收应付总额的 62%；而内资企业更多利用预收 / 预付进行资金安排，内资预收预付占预收预付总额的 75%。

三、外汇市场运行与人民币汇率

（一）外汇市场改革和建设情况

完善银行结售汇综合头寸管理。配合4月16日扩大外汇市场人民币对美元汇率浮动幅度、增加人民币汇率弹性的改革需要，取消2010年11月初以来对银行收付实现制头寸实行的临时性下限管理，并对银行结售汇综合头寸实行正负区间管理，提高银行外汇交易和风险管理的灵活性与主动性，促进人民币汇率的价格发现。

扩大银行贵金属业务汇率敞口平盘范围。将已有银行黄金业务汇率敞口平盘的政策适用范围扩大至白银、铂金等其他贵金属，便利银行为客户提供贵金属投资服务品种，支持藏金于民。

便利中小金融机构参与外汇市场。减免村镇银行进入银行间外汇市场的交易费用，发挥外汇支农作用。简化银行间外汇市场外汇掉期和货币掉期业务的市场准入管理，并增加货币掉期业务的本金交换形式，进一步推动金融服务实体经济。

扩大个人本外币兑换特许业务试点范围。简化准入管理，鼓励品牌连锁经营，强调风险防控，推动建立以银行为主体、外币代兑机构和特许经营机构为补充的规范、有效、多样的个人本外币兑换市场体系。

（二）人民币汇率走势

人民币对美元汇率双向波动增强。2012年6月末，人民币对美元汇率中间价为6.3249元/美元，较2011年末贬值0.4%（见图3-1），2005年人民币汇率形成机制改革以来累计升值30.9%。上半年117个交易日中，人民币对美元汇率中间价隔日波幅日均55个基点（2011年全年日均波幅43个基点），中间价56个交易日隔日升值，61个交易日隔日贬值，参考篮子货币汇率变动更加显现。上半年，人民币对欧元、日元汇率中间价分别升值3.7%和1.8%。

人民币汇率趋向合理均衡水平。2012年上半年，银行间外汇市场人民币对美元即期交易价相对中间价的日间最大波幅日均为0.34%，高于2011年全年的0.18%。4月16日扩大人民币汇率波幅后进一步扩大至0.53%，最高接近1%的浮动区间上限（见图3-2）。在央行大幅减少外汇干预后，市场供求决定汇率、汇率调节市场供求的自主机制更加稳固。上半年，境内外远期市场人民币对美元汇率时升时贬、有强有弱（见图3-3），6月末境内银行间远期市场、境外无本金交割远期市场（NDF）和香港可交割远期市场1年期价格隐含的人民币贬值幅度分别为1.2%、1.4%、1.9%，远低于2008年国际金融危机时7%的高点，符合当前人民币紧、美元松的本外币利差水平，而非单纯的汇率预期。这表明，当前人民币汇率处于市场认可的合理水平，不存在大规模看空人民币。

图 3-1

2012年上半年人民币对美元、欧元和日元汇率中间价走势

数据来源：中国外汇交易中心。

图 3-2

2012年上半年银行间外汇市场人民币对美元即期交易价波幅

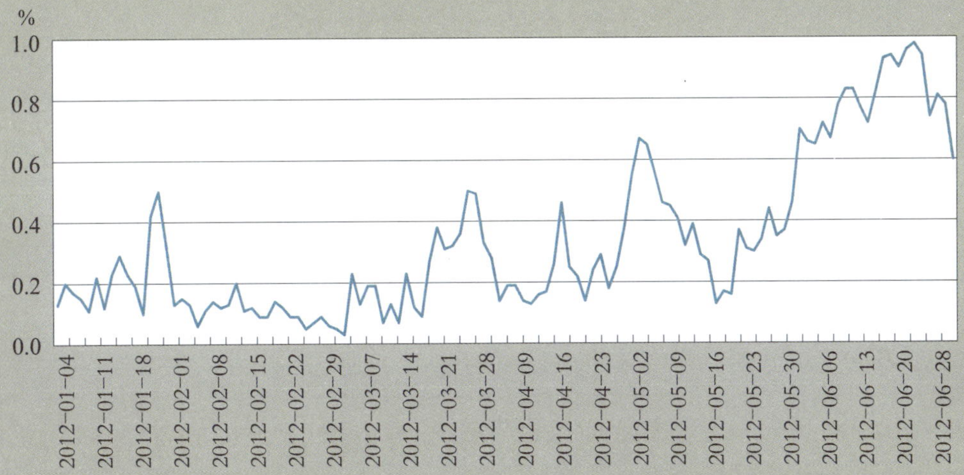

注：日间交易价相对当日中间价的最大波幅。
数据来源：中国外汇交易中心。

图 3-3

2012 年上半年境内外远期市场 1 年期人民币对美元升贬值幅度

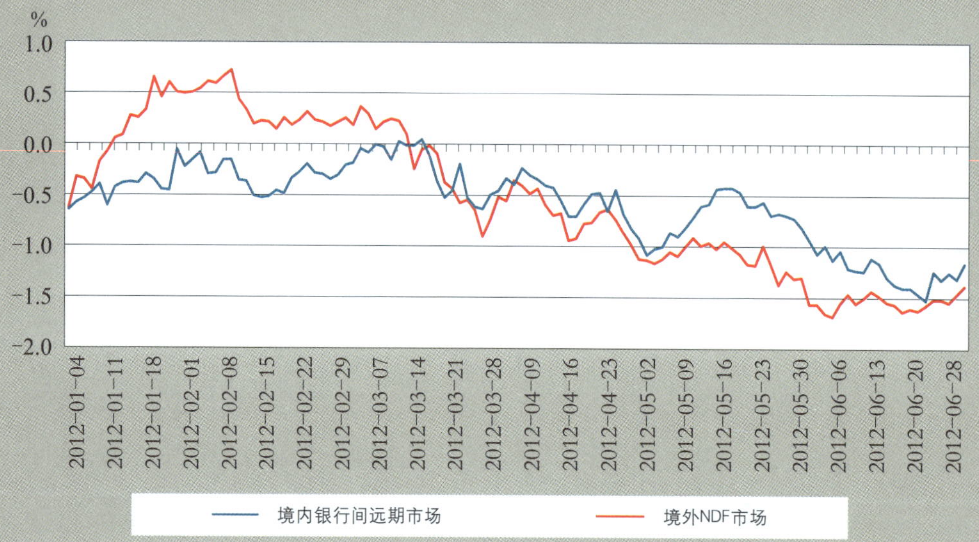

数据来源：中国外汇交易中心、路透。

人民币有效汇率升值。根据国际清算银行数据，2012 年上半年人民币对一篮子货币的名义有效汇率累计升值 1.6%，扣除通货膨胀因素的实际有效汇率累计升值 0.9%，在国际清算银行监测的 61 个经济体货币中，升值幅度分别居第 16 位和第 22

图 3-4

1994—2012 年上半年人民币有效汇率走势

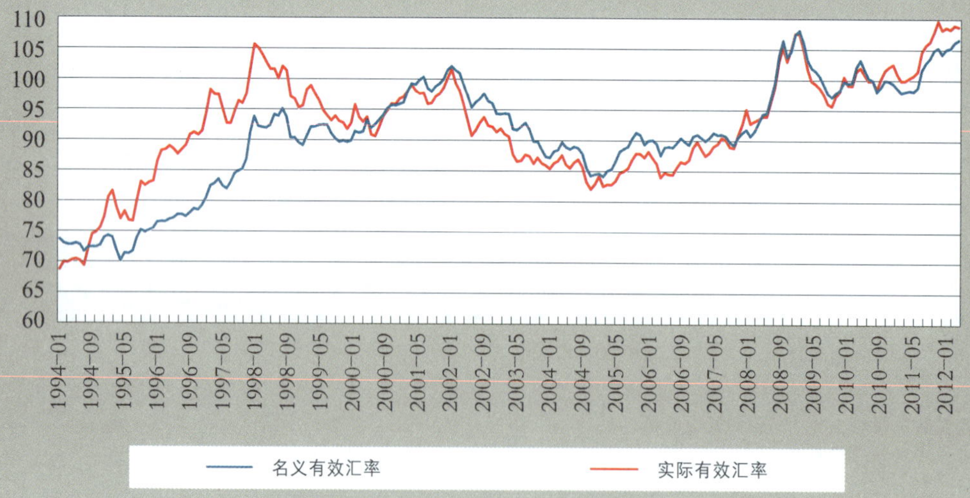

数据来源：国际清算银行。

位，人民币在新兴市场货币中表现稳定。2005 年人民币汇率形成机制改革以来，人民币名义和实际有效汇率累计分别升值 23.1% 和 30.4%（见图 3-4）。

专栏 5

我国与其他“金砖国家”国际收支状况比较

国际上测度跨境资本流动状况，主要用国际收支平衡表的资本和金融项目（不含储备资产变动），包括直接投资、证券投资和其他投资。2005—2011 年，中国、印度、巴西资本净流入累计分别为 0.96 万亿、0.39 万亿和 0.40 万亿美元，俄罗斯资本累计净流出 0.17 万亿美元（见表 C5-1）。具体比较各国的国际收支状况可以发现，虽然同为“金砖”，但彼此“成色”却不同。

表 C5-1　2005—2011 年“金砖国家”资本项目状况　　单位：亿美元

	外国直接投资	对外直接投资	外国证券投资	对外证券投资	外国其他投资	对外其他投资
中国	11 509	−2 631	1 696	−1 207	6 140	−5 936
	8 878		489		204	
印度	2 001	−1 017	1 142	−14	1 300	−41
	984		1 128		1 753	
俄罗斯	3 053	−3 009	−576	25	3 014	−4 209
	44		−551		−1 195	
巴西	2 546	−587	1 924	187	1 439	−1 492
	1 959		2 111		−53	

注：正值表示资金流入，负值表示资金流出。
数据来源：国家外汇管理局、俄罗斯中央银行、环亚数据库。

我国资本流入具有较强的稳定性。外国直接投资是“金砖国家”最主要的资本流入渠道，我国尤为明显。在流量方面，2005—2011 年，外国直接投资累计净流入 1.15 万亿美元，占同期我国资本净流入的 120%，超过印度、俄罗斯、巴西流入总和；外国证券投资累计净流入 1 696 亿美元，仅占我国同期资本净流入的 18%，印度、巴西分别为 31%、47%。在存量方面，2011 年末外国直接投资占我国全部对外负债的 61%，明显高于印度、俄罗斯、巴西（分别为 32%、41%、44%），而证券投资的比重仅为 8%，远低于上述三国（分别为 24%、21%、44%）。跨境资金流入以稳定性高的外国直接投资为主，意味着即使外部环境恶化，对风险最敏感、波动性大的证券投资撤离我国的影响也低于其他新兴市场。

全球银行业对我国净敞口规模偏低。过去几年，我国在跨境商业和银行信用（记入国际收支平衡表中其他投资的贸易信贷、贷款和存款）活动渠道的资金有进有出，2005—2011年累计净流入347亿美元，同期印度、俄罗斯、巴西净流入分别为1 753亿、705亿和143亿美元。2011年末，我国跨境商业和银行信用活动项下对外净负债863亿美元，同期上述三国分别为对外净负债2 697亿、1 126亿和596亿美元。根据国际清算银行的统计，2011年末全球银行业对我国债权来自欧洲和美国的比重（70.1%）低于印度（73.1%）、俄罗斯（94.9%）、巴西（93.3%），而国内债务人以银行部门为主（各国的比重分别为47.2%、27.3%、26.6%、14.4%），企业直接借债相对较少。这意味着欧美银行业的去杠杆化对我国的影响低于其他新兴市场，特别是实体经济可以从银行体系获得一定程度的中间缓冲。

我国贸易状况好于其他“金砖国家”。贸易状况是衡量一国对外支付能力和长期偿债能力的重要指标，特别是对于依赖资本流入弥补国内储蓄缺口的国家，如果流入的资金不能有效提升国际竞争力和改善贸易状况，将侵蚀偿债能力并最终导致债务性资本的撤离。实际上，贸易赤字与短期资本流入的结合通常被视为货币危机甚至是金融危机的前兆，1997年亚洲金融危机中的泰国就面临这种状况。相对于印度非石油贸易连续8年逆差、出口成熟度低于亚洲平均水平和俄罗斯、巴西的贸易顺差依赖于大宗商品出口，我国具有显著的贸易优势，如改革开放与稳定的营商环境、完整的制造产业链等，这使得过去10年间形成的出口竞争力在短期内既不会消失，也难以大规模外移。

回顾过去几年的国际收支状况，我国的跨境资本流动贴近实体经济活动，对于外部冲击具有较强的韧性，因此也避免了人民币汇率大起大落。2012年上半年，人民币对一篮子货币的名义有效汇率升值1.6%，巴西、印度、俄罗斯和南非四国货币分别贬值8.4%、贬值4.7%、贬值1.3%和升值0.1%。

（三）外汇市场交易

2012年上半年，人民币外汇市场累计成交4.48万亿美元，日均成交383亿美元，较上年全年日均增长 8.2%。其中，银行对客户市场和银行间外汇市场分别成交 1.55 万亿和 2.93 万亿美元[①]（见表 3–1）。

即期外汇交易平稳增长。上半年，银行对客户即期结售汇（不含远期履约）累计 1.36 万亿美元，较 2011 年全年日均增长 5.1%；银行间即期外汇市场累计成交 1.73 万亿美元，日均成交 148 亿美元，较 2011 年全年日均增长 1.3%。2012 年上半年，即期交易在外汇市场交易总量中的比重降至历史最低的 68.8%（见图 3–5），显示随着人民币汇率弹性增强，汇率衍生产品的市场需求上升。

图 3–5

2006—2012 年上半年即期交易在外汇市场交易总量中的比重

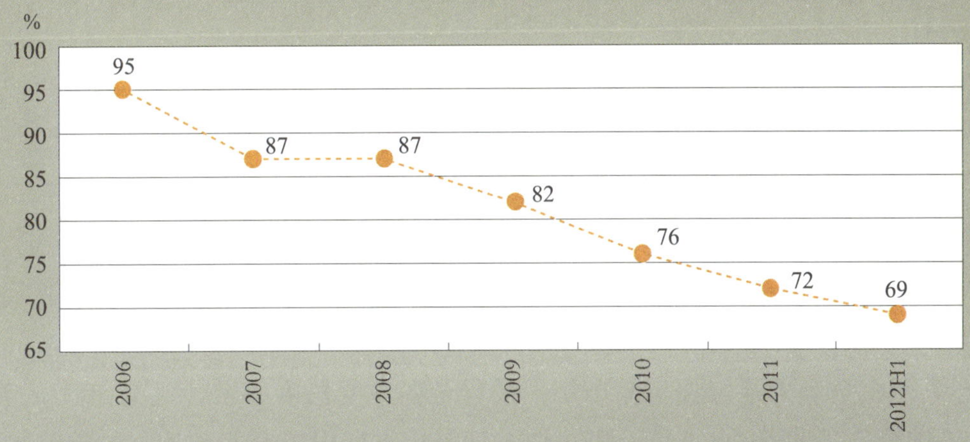

数据来源：国家外汇管理局、中国外汇交易中心。

远期外汇交易下降。上半年，银行对客户远期结售汇累计签约 1 731 亿美元，其中结汇和售汇分别为 839 亿和 892 亿美元，较 2011 年全年日均分别下降 6.7%、8.5%、5%，企业由净结汇转向净售汇（见图 3–6）。同期，银行间远期外汇市场累计成交 645 亿美元，日均成交 5.5 亿美元，较 2011 年全年日均下降 37.3%，主要原因是 4 月份取消银行收付实现制头寸下限管理后，银行对客户远期交易的敞口平盘方式回归即期 + 掉期，银行间远期交易需求减少。

外汇和货币掉期交易大幅增长。上半年，银行对客户外汇和货币掉期累计签约 156 亿美元，较 2011 年全年日均增长 1.3 倍，其中近端结汇 / 远端售汇和近端售汇 / 远端结汇的交易量比重分别为 6.3% 和 93.7%，反映出企业通过掉期业务的

① 银行对客户市场采用客户买卖外汇总额，银行间外汇市场采用单边交易量，以下同。

融资功能，将人民币资金转换为外币资金使用。同期，银行间外汇和货币掉期市场累计成交 1.14 万亿美元，日均成交 97.2 亿美元，较 2011 年日均增长 33.9%。

图 3-6

2006—2012 年上半年银行对客户远期结售汇业务量

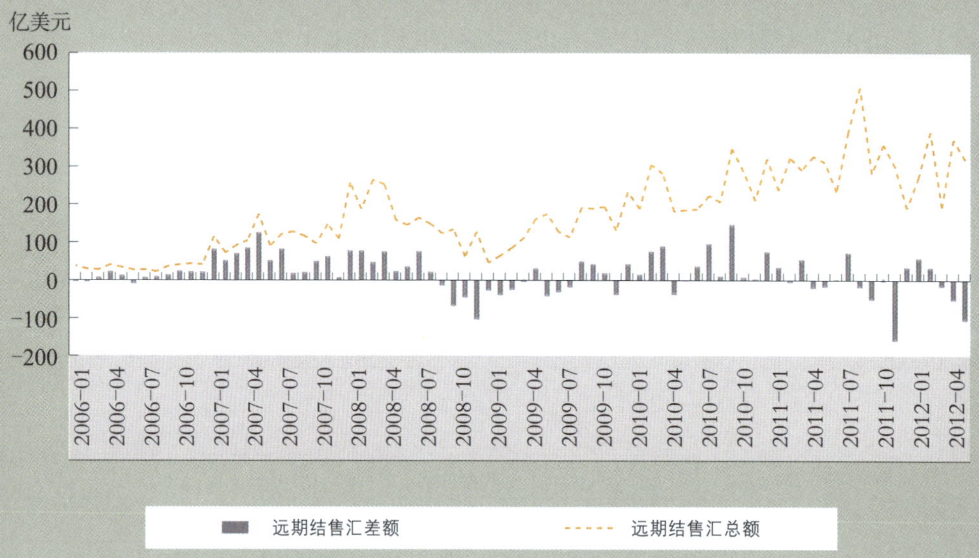

数据来源：国家外汇管理局。

外汇期权交易大幅增长。上半年，银行对客户期权市场累计成交 59.1 亿美元，是 2011 年全年交易量的 6.8 倍，以企业办理零成本期权组合业务为主，单纯买入期权较少；银行间期权市场累计成交 10.8 亿美元，超过 2011 年全年交易量。外汇期权交易趋向活跃，反映出随着人民币汇率弹性增强，期权相对于远期所具有的灵活管理汇率双向波动风险的吸引力逐渐显现。

表 3-1　2012 年上半年人民币外汇市场交易概况

交易品种	交易量（亿美元）
即期	**30 861**
银行对客户市场	13 603
银行间外汇市场	17 258
远期	**2 376**
银行对客户市场	1 731
银行间外汇市场	645
其中：3 个月（含）以下	387

续表

交易品种	交易量（亿美元）
3个月至1年（含）	153
1年以上	106
外汇和货币掉期	**11 528**
银行对客户市场	156
银行间外汇市场	11 372
其中：3个月（含）以下	10 156
3个月至1年（含）	1 188
1年以上	28
期权	**69.9**
银行对客户市场	59.1
其中：外汇看涨 / 人民币看跌	29.1
外汇看跌 / 人民币看涨	30
银行间外汇市场	10.8
其中：外汇看涨 / 人民币看跌	5.8
外汇看跌 / 人民币看涨	5.1
其中：3个月（含）以下	7.9
3个月至1年（含）	2.9
1年以上	0
合计	**44 835**
其中：银行对客户市场	15 549
银行间外汇市场	29 286
其中：即期	30 861
远期	2 376
外汇和货币掉期	11 528
期权	69.9

注：数据均为单边交易额，采用四舍五入原则。
数据来源：国家外汇管理局、中国外汇交易中心。

银行间外币对交易小幅下降。上半年，9个外币对买卖累计成交折合428亿美元，日均成交3.7亿美元，较2011年日均下降5.7%。其中，即期交易作为最大交易品种累计成交折合362亿美元，日均成交3.1亿美元，较2011年日均下降11.9%。在交易币种分布，以美元/港元、欧元/美元为主（见图3-7），符合国际外汇市场格局和内地与香港之间特有的经济联系。

图 3-7

2005—2012 年上半年银行间外汇市场外币对即期交易的币种构成

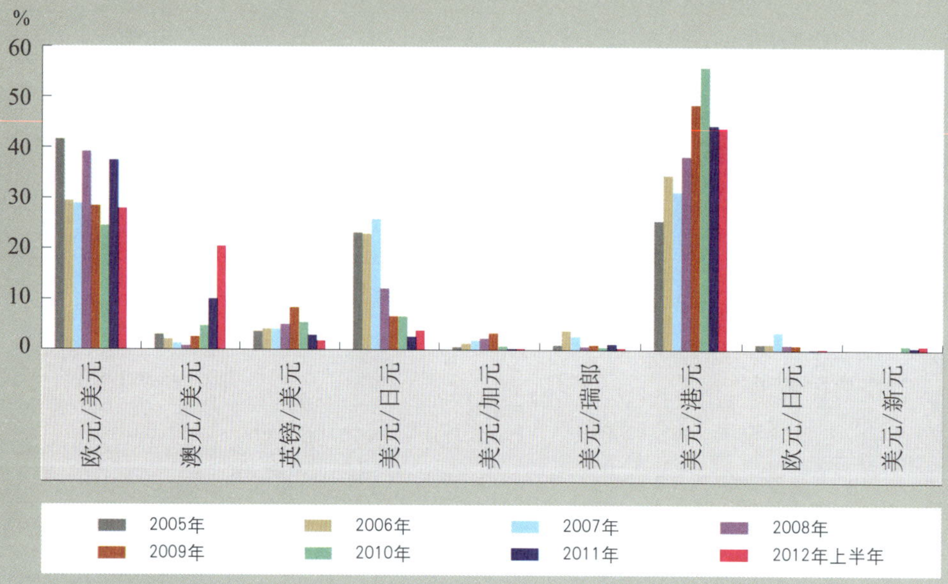

数据来源：中国外汇交易中心。

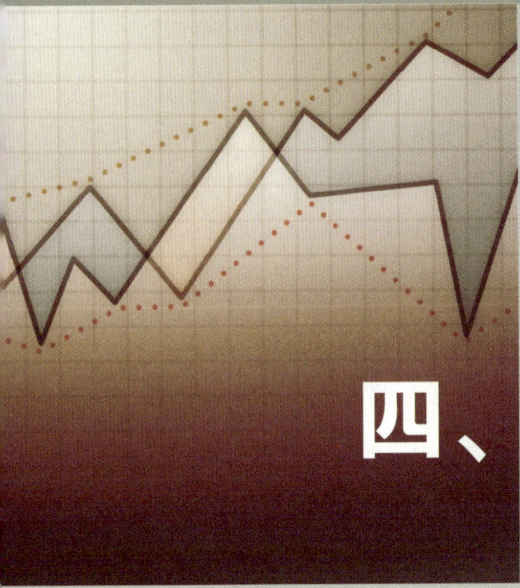

四、国际收支形势展望和政策取向

当前，国际收支顺差减少、外汇储备增长放缓，符合国家宏观调控方向，有利于促进对外经济平衡。随着人民币汇率形成机制不断完善，以及央行外汇干预大幅减少，我国经常项目顺差、资本项目逆差的国际收支平衡格局将成为常态，有利于推进藏汇于民。在世界经济缓慢复苏、国际金融动荡加剧的背景下，我国作为开放程度越来越高的经济体，跨境资本流动受到影响在所难免。当国际收支、人民币汇率趋向合理均衡水平后，跨境资本双向波动也不可避免。我国经济增长相对较快、货物贸易持续顺差、外汇储备规模雄厚，且外资主要是稳定性较高的直接投资而非波动性较大的证券投资，能够承受跨境资本流动的冲击。

2012 年下半年我国国际收支有望保持基本平衡。外部环境继续存在许多不稳定、不确定的因素，如美国经济可能小幅向好，但仍面临“财政悬崖”带来的财政紧缩问题；欧元区总体处于去杠杆化的初级阶段，欧债危机仍可能不断深化；受外围经济环境影响，新兴市场经济体面临供给和需求两方面压力；地缘政治突发事件也不容忽视，等等。但一些有利于我国国际收支平衡的积极因素也正在逐步积累：一是国家把稳增长放在更加重要的位置，近期出台的一系列预调微调政策将有助于提振市场信心，保持经济平稳增长。二是鉴于世界经济低迷，国际大宗商品价格回落压低国内进口成本，下半年我国有可能继续保持较大的货物贸易顺差。三是各主要经济体将更加注重增长，相关国家和地区也仍有一定资源和决心防止债务危机走向最坏情形。总体来看，只要国内外不发生重大突发事件，全年我国的国际收支仍有望实现基本平衡。

专栏 6

欧债危机的现状与影响

欧债危机始于 2009 年的希腊主权债务危机。在希腊宣布无法按期偿还主权债务后，欧洲长期存在的人口老龄化、社保高福利化、劳动力市场僵化、货币一体化但财政独立化等固有的结构性矛盾集中爆发，由于经济政策协调成本高昂且效率低下，经过不断演化发酵，欧债危机目前已发展成包括主权债务危机、银行业危机、经济政治危机和社会危机在内的全方位、系统性危机。

2012 年以来，欧债危机大致经历了好转、恶化、趋缓等阶段。第一季度，欧洲央行推出了总额达 5 295 亿欧元的第二轮三年期再融资操作（LTRO），欧盟峰会缔结了《稳定、协调和治理条约》财政契约以强化欧盟区财政纪律和监督，缓解了欧洲银行业流动性紧缺状况，提升了市场信心。但进入第二季度，随着西班牙财政赤字问题逐渐恶化和欧洲银行业资本充足率不达标等新问题陆续浮现，西班牙、意大利等国国债价格出现暴跌，持有较多欧债头寸的欧洲多家银行被降级，欧债危机再度恶化。为应对危机，欧盟出台了向西班牙提供1 000亿欧元的救助贷款，推进银行联盟一体化，推出1 200亿欧元促增长方案等一系列措施。然而，这些措施并未解决根本问题，仅仅缓和了危机进程。7月份希腊救助谈判陷入僵局，西班牙地方政府债务问题爆发。9月份荷兰将要举行大选，由于荷兰民众对于欧盟紧缩方案普遍不满，大选结果可能导致新政府偏离欧盟预算目标约束，从而导致荷兰失去AAA级信用评级。9月份德国最高法院将对欧洲稳定机制（Europe Stability Mechanism，ESM）进行裁决，一旦裁决结果不为民众所接受，可能触发德国全民公投。欧债危机前景再度蒙上阴影。

欧盟是世界第一大经济体，欧元区是世界最大的单一货币区，欧元是仅次于美元的第二大国际储备货币，此次欧债危机对欧洲乃至世界经济金融的影响巨大。欧债危机以来，欧盟经济增长率预计将从2010年的2.0%下滑到2012年的0，欧盟失业率从2010年的9.7%攀升到了2012年6月的10.4%。欧盟政府债务总量占GDP比重从2010年的80.0%上升到了83.4%。随着欧洲各国经济陷入衰退和主权信用评级不断降低，欧债国家普遍陷入了财政紧缩—经济衰退—债务负担加重—财政再度紧缩的恶性循环。从国际经济往来方面看，欧盟对外贸易出现下降，这也极大地影响到了欧盟各贸易伙伴国。从金融市场方面看，欧元区稳定性受到冲击，2012年6月欧元对美元汇率从2010年底的1.3583贬值到1.2814，欧洲股票债券市场等出现剧烈震荡，持有大量欧债头寸的欧洲多家金融机构资产蒙受巨大损失，银行贷款业务陷入停滞。经济金融危机也对欧洲政治、社会局面造成不利影响，欧盟内部各国矛盾冲突不断，欧洲一体化进程受到争议。长期的经济不景气和失业问题导致危机中的欧洲民众不满，政府更迭，社会动荡。

2012年下半年，外汇管理部门将按照党中央、国务院的统一部署，把握好稳中求进的主基调，把稳增长放在更加重要的位置，坚守风险底线，进一步提高外汇管理服务实体经济和维护国家经济金融安全的能力。一是坚持防风险不放松，密切跟踪跨境资金流动走势，完善政策预案，防范化解外汇管理领域风险隐患。二是促进贸易投资便利化，做好货物贸易外汇管理制度改革全国推广，进一步简化跨境直接投资管理，稳步推进合格境内机构投资者制度和合格境外机构投资者制度发展。三是加快外汇市场发展，丰富人民币外汇衍生产品，改进做市商做市机制，增强外汇市场自我调节、自求平衡的能力。四是加强和改进外汇储备经营管理，维护国家外汇资产安全。

Ⅰ. Overview of the Balance of Payments

(I) The Balance of Payments environment

In the first half of 2012, global economic growth decelerated. Economic growth in the advanced economies was weak, especially in the Euro zone, and growth in the major emerging economies dropped as well (see Chart 1–1). International financial markets continued to fluctuate: the European debt crisis subsided in the first quarter but then deteriorated in the second quarter due to political turbulence in Greece and intensified sovereign debt and banking-sector risks in Spain and Italy. The European sovereign debt crisis escalated and risk aversion in international markets increased (see Chart 1–2). The emerging economies were facing widespread capital outflows because capital flowed back to Europe or turned to safe assets, causing the stock markets and exchange rates to fluctuate in the major economies. In the second quarter, the MSCI emerging market stock index and the money index accumulated decreases of 10 percent and 5 percent respectively (see Chart 1–3). The price of bulk commodity fluctuated substantially. The NYMEX light sweet crude oil price and the LME copper price dropped significantly, by 21 percent and 12 percent respectively, by the end of June from their respective high levels around March.

Chart 1–1

Economic Growth of the Major Economies from 2007 to the First Half of 2012

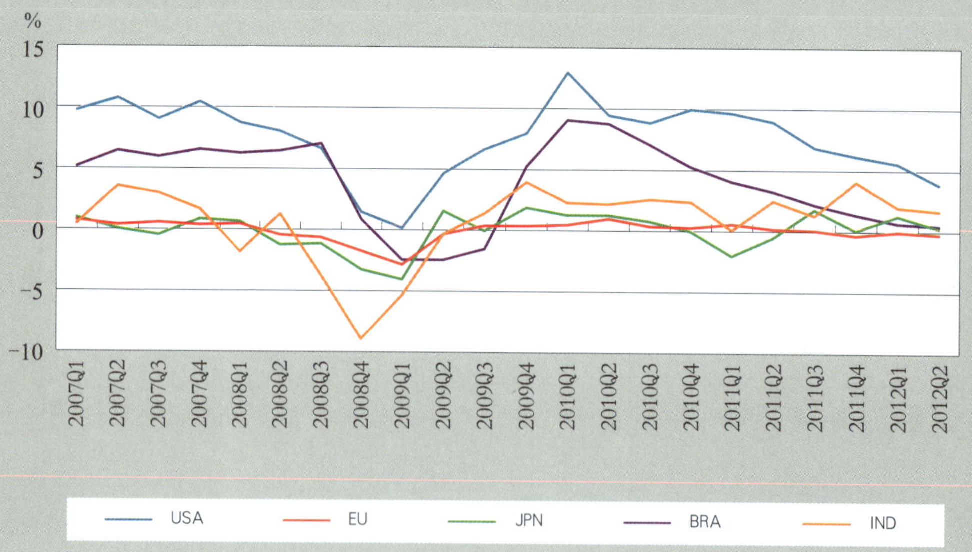

Notes: The growth rates in the United States, the Euro area, and Japan are quarterly growth rates, and the growth rates in Brazil and India are quarterly growth rates year on year.

Source: CEIC

Chart 1-2

The CDS and VIX Index of the Italian and Spanish Sovereign Debt from 2011 to the First Half of 2012

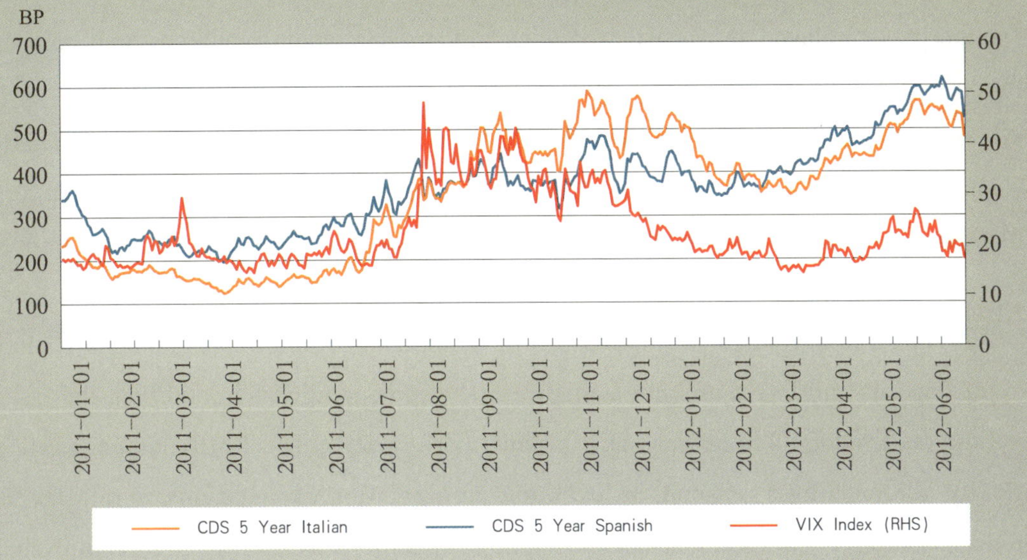

Notes: Higher CDS (Credit Default Swaps) indicate higher default risks for borrowers. A higher VIX indicates deteriorating panic in the market.

Sources: Bloomberg, Reuters.

Chart 1-3

Stock Indices and Money Indices in the Emerging Markets from 2011 to the First Half of 2012

Sources: Bloomberg, Reuters.

In the first half of 2012, China continued its policies of stimulating domestic consumption, improving the consumption capability of domestic residents, and adjusting the investment structure by encouraging private investment. In addition, the government launched measures to stabilize exports and to expand imports in order to improve the balance of payments situation. The authorities employed active fiscal policies and steady monetary policies, and paid more attention to pre-adjustment and fine-tuning policies, leading to a stabilized economy with a slowdown in growth. During the first half of 2012 the GDP growth rate was 7.8 percent, and the inflation rate dropped significantly (see Chart 1–4). The tasks of making economic structural adjustments and maintaining steady growth remained serious. The financial sector provided better support for the real sector: on two occasions the central bank cut the deposit reserve ratio for deposit-taking financial institutions by 1 percentage point, cut benchmark interest rates for deposits and loans, and intensified reverse repo operations. In addition, the tasks of preventing and reducing financial risks became more serious. The RMB exchange rate was gradually approaching a reasonable level, and appreciation expectations were alleviated. Moreover, domestic entities adjusted their financial operations by increasing foreign exchange purchasing and holding, and weakened motivations for foreign exchange financing.

Chart 1–4

The Quarterly GDP Growth Rate and the Monthly CPI Growth Rate from 2008 to the First Half of 2012

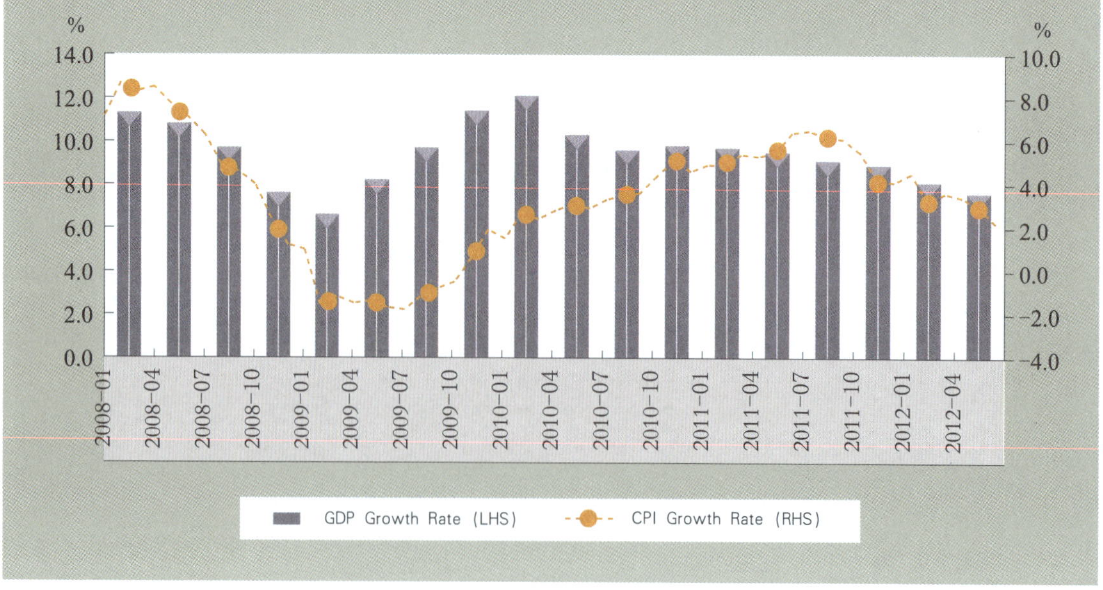

Sources: NBS.

(Ⅱ) The Main Characteristics of the Balance of Payments

The balance of payments posted twin surpluses. In the first half of 2012, the current account surplus totaled USD 77.2 billion, down 12 percent year on year; the capital and financial account surplus was USD 14.9 billion, down 92 percent (see Table 1–1).

Table 1–1 Structure of the BOP Surplus from 2006 to the First Half of 2012 Unit: USD 100 million

Item \ Year	2006	2007	2008	2009	2010	2011	2012H1
BOP surplus	2 811	4 474	4 607	4 417	5 247	4 228	921
Current Account surplus	2 318	3 532	4 206	2 433	2 378	2 017	772
As of BOP surplus(%)	82.5	78.9	91.3	55.1	45.3	47.7	83.9
As of GDP(%)	8.5	10.1	9.3	4.9	4.0	2.8	2.1
Capital and financial account surplus	493	942	401	1 985	2 869	2 211	149
As of BOP surplus(%)	17.5	21.1	8.7	44.9	54.7	52.3	16.1
As of GDP(%)	1.8	2.7	0.9	4.0	4.8	3.0	0.4

Sources: SAFE, NBS.

The surplus in trade in goods increased. Based on the balance-of-payments statistics, goods exports and imports totaled USD 957.7 billion and USD 844.9 billion respectively, up by 9 percent and 7 percent, resulting in a trade in goods surplus of USD 112.8 billion①, up by 29 percent year on year (see Chart 1–5).

The deficit in trade in services increased further. In the first half of the year, the revenue in trade in services amounted to USD 90.3 billion, the same level as that in the first half of 2011; payments totaled USD 130.5 billion, increasing by 19 percent year on year; and the deficit in trade in services surged by 104 percent to USD 40.3 billion. In the first half of the year, the surplus in trade in goods and trade in services totaled USD 72.6 billion, rising by 7 percent year on year. The ratio of the surplus to GDP was 2 percent, down by 0.2 percentage point year on year (see Chart 1–6).

① The BOP statistics and the statistics of the General Administration of Customs regarding trade in goods can be reconciled by the following: First, imports based on the BOP statistics equal 95 percent of imports based on custom statistics by quoting the CIF and assuming 5 percent to be insurance and freight. Second, the BOP statistics include goods repatriation, goods purchased at ports, and smuggled goods which are deducted from the import and export returns.

Chart 1-5

Main Items Under the Current Account from 2001 to the First Half of 2012

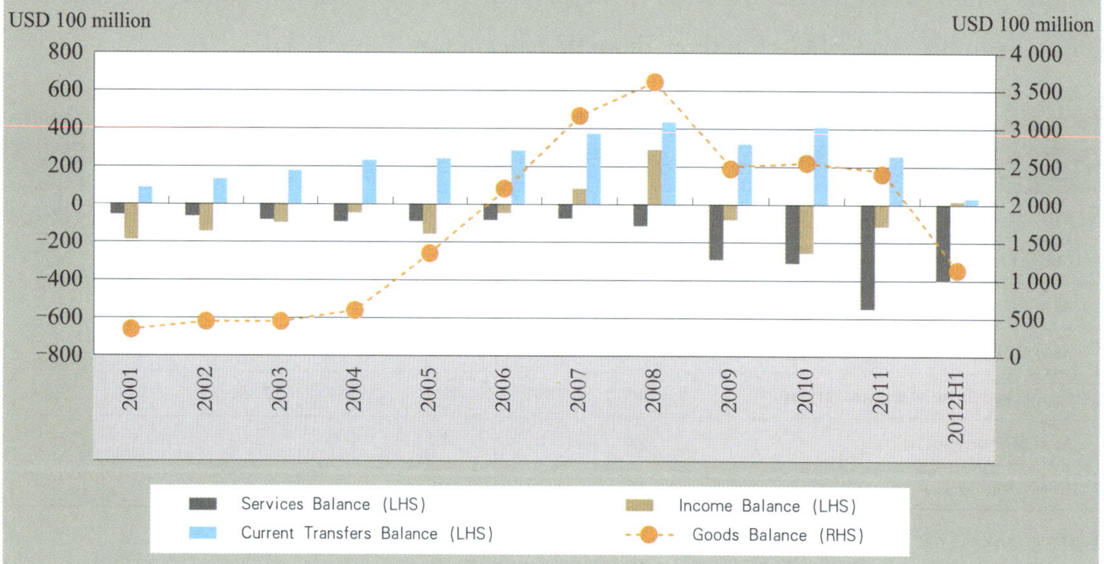

Sources: SAFE.

Chart 1-6

The Ratio of the Balance of Trade in Goods and Trade in Services to GDP, from 1994 to the First Half of 2012

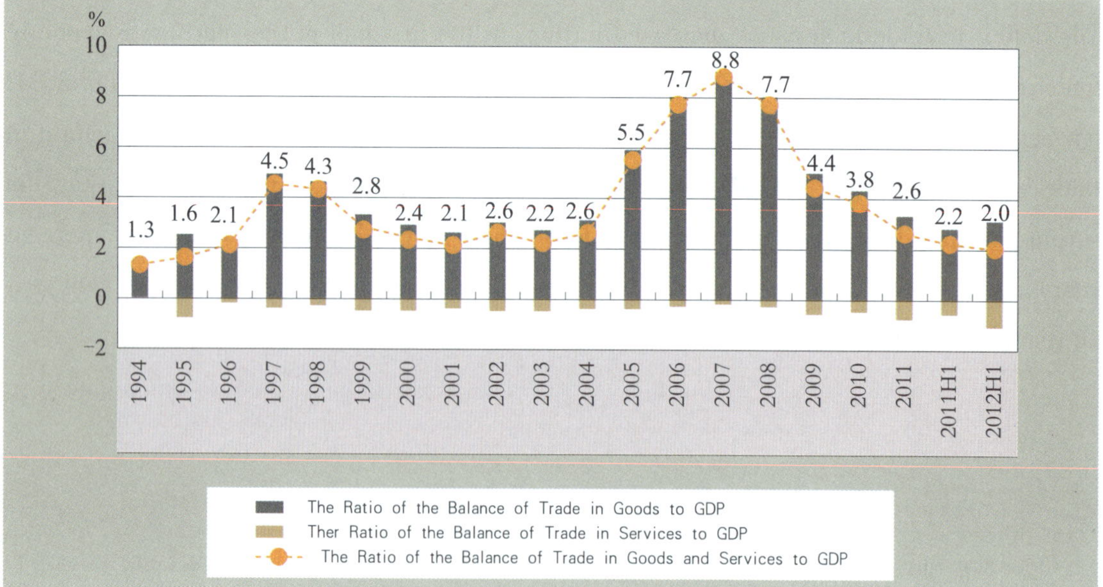

Sources: SAFE, NBS.

The income item achieved a surplus. In the first half of the year, income and payment totaled USD 90.2 billion and USD 88.5 billion respectively, each increasing by 22 percent year on year and resulting in a surplus of USD 1.6 billion, a drop of 11 percent. In particular, investment income and payments increased by 24 percent and 23 percent year on year, and their deficit surged by 7 percent to USD 5.7 billion. Excluding the foreign-funded enterprises' retained earnings and unremitted profits, in the first half of the year the profit of foreign shareholder remittances increased by 14 percent year on year and there was no evidence of any abnormalities.

Direct investment continued to post a large surplus. Based on the balance of payments statistics, direct investment recorded a surplus of USD 90 billion in the first half of the year, down 3 percent year on year. In particular, inward direct investment recorded a net inflow of USD 118.1 billion,① up by 6 percent, and outward direct investment recorded a net outflow of USD 28.1 billion, up by 53 percent (see Chart 1–7).

Chart 1–7

Major Items Under the Capital and Financial Account from 2001 to the First Half of 2012

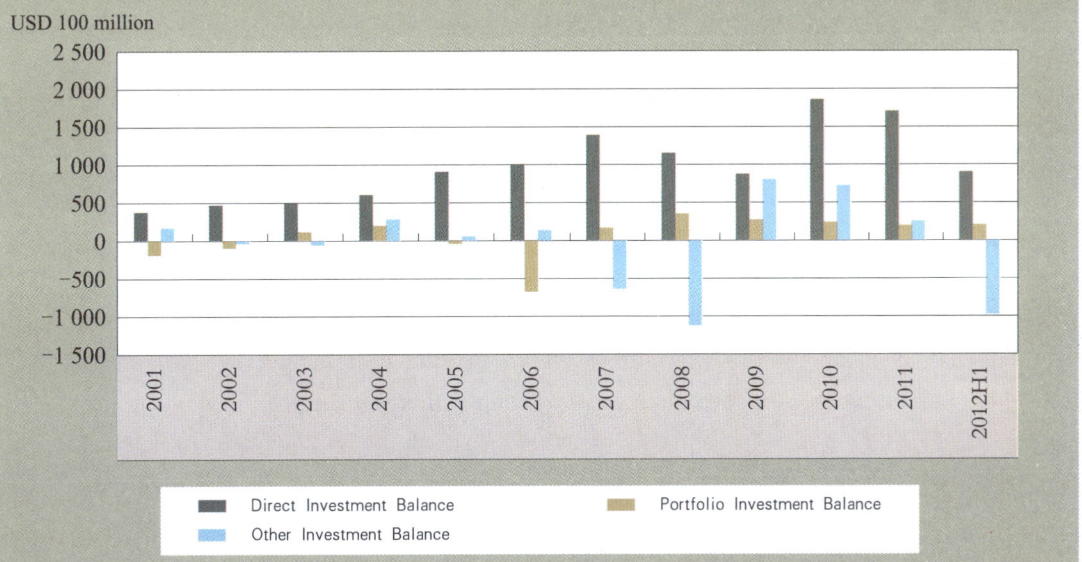

Sources: SAFE.

① The BOP statistics and the statistics of the Ministry of Commerce regarding FDI can be reconciled by the following: The BOP statistics include unpaid and unremitted profits of foreign shareholders in foreign-funded enterprises, loans from shareholders, FDI in the financial sector, real property purchased by nonresidents, and so forth.

Net inflows of portfolio investment rose rapidly. In the first half of the year, net inflows of portfolio investment totaled USD 20.4 billion, increasing by 1.4 times year on year. In particular, outward portfolio investment recorded a net inflow of USD 5.9 billion, from posting a net inflow of USD 0.5 billion in the first half of 2011. Inward portfolio investment posted a net inflow of USD 14.5 billion, up by 84 percent.

Other investment recorded significant net outflows. In the first half of the year, net outflows of other investment totaled USD 97.9 billion, from a net inflow of USD 79.8 billion in the first half of 2011. Influenced by both domestic and external factors, including RMB exchange rate fluctuations and brewing of the European debt crisis, Chinese enterprises were more willing to hold foreign currency, leading to increased foreign currency deposits and loans as well as to increased external loans by enterprises. As a result, other investment assets increased by USD 162.3 billion, rising by 109 percent year on year. In the meantime, growth in external borrowing by domestic enterprises and banks as well as nonresident deposits and loans decelerated, leading to an increase of USD 64.4 billion under the item of other investment liabilities, down by 59 percent year on year.

Box 1

How to Evaluate the Growth of Foreign Currency Deposits

Since 2012, foreign currency deposits by banks have surged rapidly (see Chart C1-1). In the first half of the year, they increased by a cumulative USD 130.1 billion, USD 99.4 billion more than the increase in the first half of 2011. As analyzed, with weakened RMB appreciation expectations, this was mainly driven mainly by enterprise adjustments to financial operations. There was no evidence to indicate that institutions and individuals were accumulating foreign currency assets driven by shorting the RMB.

The growth of foreign currency deposits resulted from fiscal adjustments by enterprises. In the past several years, enterprises have tended to hold domestic-currency assets and foreign-currency liabilities due to RMB appreciation expectations and it was reasonable to short the USD. However, with the more balanced BOP and the reasonable equilibrium level of the RMB exchange rate, and under the condition of the interest rate and exchange rate spread between domestic and foreign currency at this moment, enterprises began to cut their previous USD position and to no longer overly short the USD. The main operations included: first, enterprises received RMB payments from foreign banks by providing collateral in foreign currency deposits via foreign currency swaps; second, enterprises received USD payments from foreign banks by providing collateral for their own foreign currency deposits. According to our incomplete survey, cross-border trade financing of domestic enterprises increased by nearly USD 50 billion through payments by foreign banks, forward letters of credit issued by domestic banks, and overseas guarantees, while foreign currency cash deposits grew by USD 58.3 billion. Foreign currency cash deposits increased more than cross-border trade financing, indicating that enterprises were gradually substituting foreign currency cash deposits for RMB cash deposits, and they were covering their unhedged previous position of the USD from cross-border financing. The movement was reasonable and a normal and positive performance by enterprises to adapt to the new environment, and it was not motivated by a pure RMB depreciation expectation without real demand to build the USD long position. In fact, the main source of foreign currency deposit growth was enterprises, and foreign currency deposits of individuals increased by only USD 2.1 billion during the first half of 2012.

The growth of foreign currency deposits was driven by domestic and foreign currency pricing by banks. Recently, some domestic banks overpriced foreign currency deposits due to lagged adjustments, causing the interest rate spread between domestic and foreign currency to be substantially lower than the USD appreciation in the forward foreign exchange market. Enterprises exchanged RMB deposits for USD currency by retaining their foreign currency revenue or by foreign currency swap transactions, and at the same time sold forward USD to gain risk-free arbitrage; otherwise enterprises would sterilize according to interest rate parity and exchange rate parity. Such hedging increased USD liquidity in the banking sector, lowered the USD interest rate, and expanded the USD appreciation in the forward foreign exchange market. This indicated that the one-way appreciation expectation of the RMB was weakened, and the pricing mechanism of the interest rate and exchange rate spread in the domestic market became normalized, making the forward exchange rate reflect the interest rate spread instead of the appreciation expectation.

In the first half of the year, domestic foreign currency loans increased by USD 31.9 billion, which was far less than the growth of foreign currency deposits, implying that the banking sector had to invest its foreign currency position in external loans, investment, and lending. This was recorded as an increase in the banking sector's foreign assets and an outflow of the BOP capital and financial account. The increased foreign currency deposits by enterprises continued to circulate in the domestic financial sector and to transfer from corporations to banks, constituting so-called foreign exchange assets held by nonofficial sectors instead of capital flight.

Chart C1-1

Foreign Currency Deposits and Loans of Financial Institutions from 2008 to the First Half of 2012

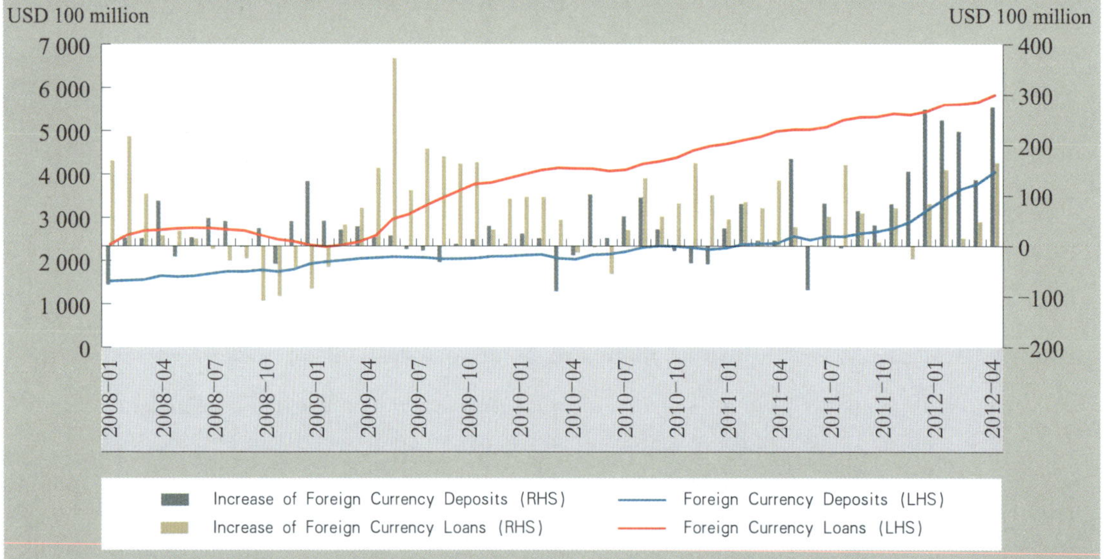

Sources: PBC.

The accumulation of foreign reserves decelerated. In the first half of year 2012, China's international reserves grew by USD 62.9 billion, excluding valuation factors such as the exchange rate and the asset price, down by 78 percent year on year. In particular, foreign reserve assets increased by USD 63.6 billion, a decrease of USD 217.4 billion from the cumulative foreign reserve assets in the first half of 2011. By the end of June, outstanding foreign reserves totaled USD 3.24 trillion (see Chart 1–8) and the net position in the IMF decreased by USD 800 million.

Chart 1-8

Increases and Balance in the Foreign Reserves Position from 2001 to the First Half of 2012

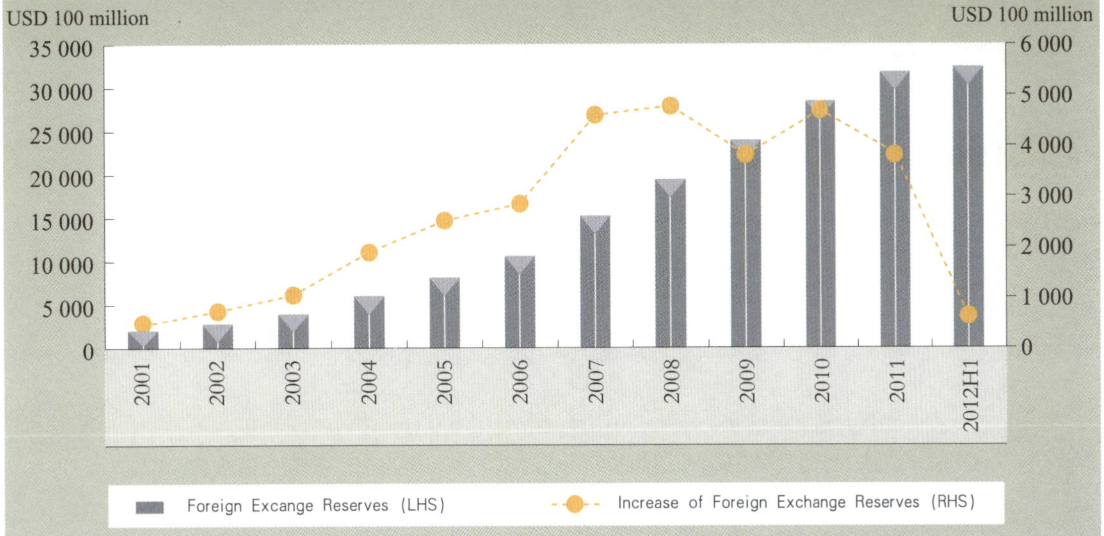

Notes: The chart indicates the growth of foreign reserves due to transactions excluding valuation factors.

Sources: SAFE.

Box 2

Outstanding Funds of the Central Bank for Foreign Exchange and the Accumulation of Foreign Reserves

Outstanding funds for foreign exchange changed by two factors: one was the RMB issued or withdrawn by the central bank via foreign exchange transactions, and the other was RMB issuances from the sale of foreign exchange from foreign reserve income.

Fluctuations in the foreign reserves are presented in two ways: One is the foreign reserve asset change in the balance of payments, which includes both the foreign reserve change resulting from the central bank's foreign exchange transactions and investment income. The other is the variation in outstanding foreign reserves, which includes not only changes in foreign reserve assets based on the BOP statistics but also valuation adjustments by non-transactional factors such as the price and the exchange rate.

Therefore, based on the statistical concepts mentioned above, the outstanding foreign reserve variation is more comprehensive than the foreign reserve asset change in the balance of payments, whose coverage is wider than the change in the outstanding funds of the Central Bank for foreign exchange (see Chart C2–1).

Chart C2–1

The Relation Between the Outstanding Funds of the Central Bank for Foreign Exchange and the Change in Foreign Reserves

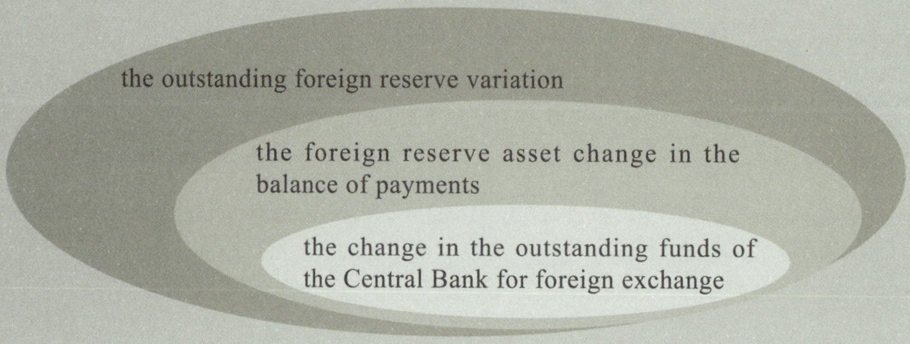

Table 1–2 China's Balance of Payments Statement in the First Half of 2012①

Unit: USD 100 million

Item	Balance	Credit	Debit
I. Current account	**772**	**11 636**	**10 863**
A. Goods and services	**726**	**10 480**	**9 754**
a. Goods	**1 128**	**9 577**	**8 449**
b. Services	**–403**	**903**	**1 305**
1. Transportation	–229	184	414
2. Travel	–218	238	456
3. Communication services	3	9	6
4. Construction services	46	61	15
5. Insurance services	–84	17	100
6. Financial services	–1	4	5

① China's balance of payments statement is compiled in accordance with the principles of the fifth edition of the *Balance of payments Manual* of the International Monetary Fund, recording all economic transactions between residents of the Chinese Mainland (excluding residents of Hong Kong SAR, Macau SAR, and Taiwan province) and nonresidents based on the principles of a double-entry system.

(Continued)

Item	Balance	Credit	Debit
7. Computer and information services	53	69	16
8. Royalties and licensing fees	−85	4	89
9. Consulting services	66	157	91
10. Advertising and public opinion polling	9	23	14
11. Audio-visual and related services	−2	1	2
12.Other business services	40	132	92
13. Government services, n.i.e.	−1	4	5
B. Income	**16**	**902**	**885**
1. Compensation of employees	73	82	9
2. Investment income	−57	820	876
C. Current transfers	**31**	**255**	**224**
1. General government	−15	4	19
2. Other sectors	46	250	205
II. Capital and financial account	**149**	**6 527**	**6 378**
A. Capital account	**24**	**25**	**1**
B. Financial account	**125**	**6 501**	**6 377**
1. Direct investment	**900**	**1 414**	**514**
1.1 Abroad	−281	100	380
1.2 In China	1 181	1 314	133
2. Portfolio investment	**204**	**310**	**106**
2.1 Assets	59	143	85
2.1.1 Equity securities	22	50	28
2.1.2 Debt securities	36	93	57
2.1.2.1 Bonds and notes	52	87	35
2.1.2.2 Money market instruments	−16	6	22
2.2 Liabilities	145	166	21
2.2.1 Equity securities	53	74	21
2.2.2 Debt securities	92	92	0
2.2.2.1 Bonds and notes	71	71	0
2.2.2.2 Money market instruments	21	21	0
3. Other investment	**−979**	**4 778**	**5 757**
3.1 Assets	−1 623	265	1 887
3.1.1 Trade credits	−332	4	336
Long-term	−7	0	7
Short-term	−326	4	330
3.1.2 Loans	−431	7	438
Long-term	−183	0	183
Short-term	−248	7	255
3.1.3 Currency and deposits	−967	146	1 113

(Continued)

Item	Balance	Credit	Debit
3.1.4 Other assets	108	108	0
Long-term	0	0	0
Short-term	108	108	0
3.2 Liabilities	644	4 513	3 870
3.2.1 Trade credits	409	409	0
Long-term	7	7	0
Short-term	402	402	0
3.2.2 Loans	379	3 394	3 015
Long-term	87	245	158
Short-term	292	3 149	2 857
3.2.3 Currency and deposits	-183	658	841
3.2.4 Other liabilities	39	53	14
Long-term	43	43	0
Short-term	–4	10	14
III. Reserve assets	**–629**	**121**	**750**
1. Monetary gold	0	0	0
2. Special drawing rights	–1	1	2
3. Reserve position in the fund	8	8	0
4. Foreign exchange	–636	0	636
5. Other claims	0	0	0
IV. Net errors and omissions	**–292**	**0**	**292**

Sources: SAFE.

(Ⅲ) Evaluation of the Balance of Payments

External economic activity grew steadily. In the first half of the year, balance of payments transactions totaled USD 3.54 trillion, rising by 10 percent year on year; the ratio to GDP was 98 percent, down by 5 percentage points year on year (see Chart 1–9). In particular, total trade in goods and trade in services increased by 8 percent year on year, and cross-border direct investment increased by 14 percent.

The balance of payments improved further. In the first half of 2012, the balance of payments recorded a surplus of USD 92.1 billion, down to the 2005 level and a drop of 66 percent year on year. The current account surplus to GDP was 2.1 percent, 0.7 percentage point lower year on year (see Chart 1–10). The accumulation of foreign reserves obviously decelerated, the ratio to GDP was 1.7 percent, down by 7.3 percentage points year on year.

Chart 1–9

China's Scale of BOP Transactions and the Ratio to GDP, from 1990 to the First Half of 2012

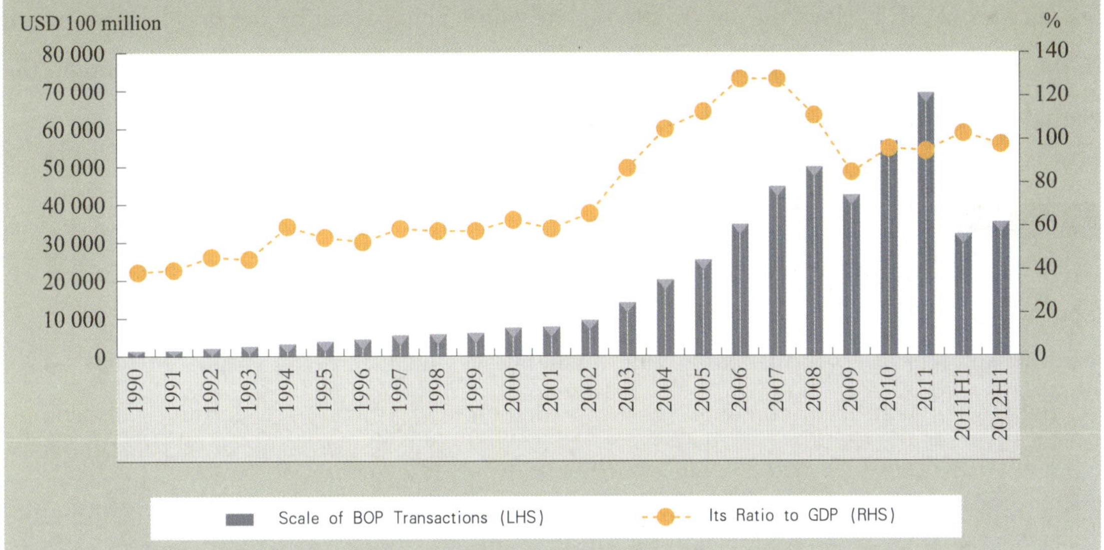

Sources: SAFE, NBS.

Chart 1–10

The Ratio of the Current Account Surplus to GDP and the Ratio of Foreign Reserve Growth to GDP from 1990 to the First Half of 2012

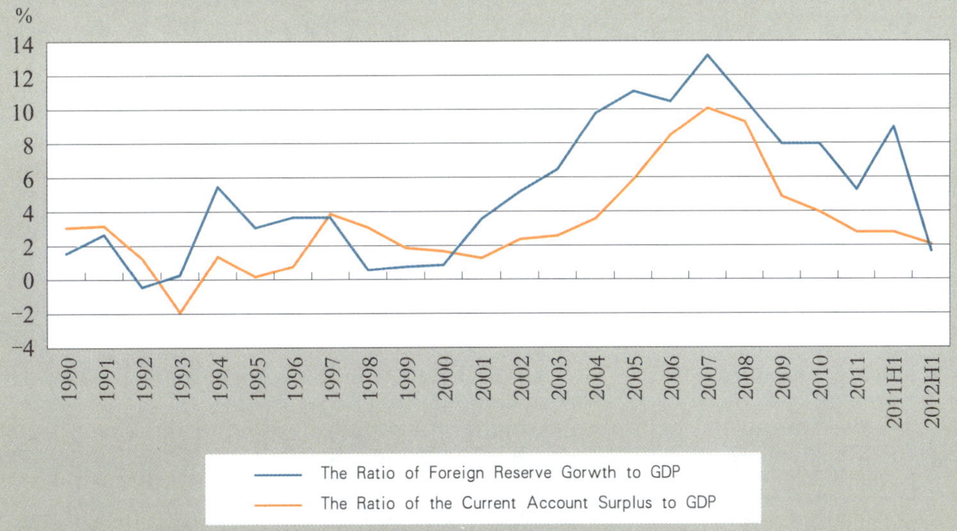

Sources: SAFE, NBS.

Cross-border capital flowed in two directions. In the first quarter of 2012, because international markets were warming, international capital flowed into China, as indicated by a surplus of USD 56.1 billion under the capital and financial account from a deficit of USD 29 billion in the last quarter of 2011. Nevertheless, in the second quarter, impacted by the decelerated growth in the real sector, the brewing of the European debt crisis, and the rising risk aversion, the capital and financial account posted a net outflow of USD 41.2 billion.

Box 3

Capital Account Deficit ≠ Massive Foreign Capital Flight

In the first half of 2012, the capital and financial account recorded a surplus of USD 14.9 billion, whereas in the second quarter it recorded a deficit of USD 41.2 billion. The deficit was driven by joint domestic and international influences instead of massive foreign capital flight. Theoretically, when the current account surplus exceeds the growth of foreign reserves, domestic institutions and individuals are exporting capital (that is, the capital and financial account deficit) and their net foreign assets are accumulating. In particular, due to the further expansion of the floating zone of the RMB exchange rate in April and to far less intervention in the foreign exchange market by the central bank, China's balance of payments situation was strengthened by the self-equilibrium mechanism, with a current account surplus and a capital and financial account deficit. More detailed BOP statistics confirm our analysis that the capital and financial account deficit came from foreign asset holdings from the central bank to domestic institutions and individuals, which are called foreign exchange assets held by the nonofficial sector. There was no significant indication of foreign capital flight.

With respect to direct investment, although they posted a surplus of USD 41.1 billion in the second quarter (see Chart C3–1) and dropped by 14 percent year on year, the decline was not driven by foreign capital withdrawals since inward direct investment withdrawals totaled USD 7.5 billion and rose by 6 percent year on year, 25 percent lower than the average growth rate of the capital and financial account outflow in the second quarter and 38 percent lower than the average quarterly growth rate of inward direct investment withdrawals since 2001. The declining direct investment surplus was driven by the growing outward direct investment (USD 19.5 billion and 17 percent growth) as more Chinese enterprises were "going abroad" given the goods price of foreign assets.

Portfolio investment recorded a surplus of USD 11.1 billion in the second quarter, 20 percent higher than the surplus in the first quarter. The main sources of the surplus were: first, outward portfolio investment recorded a net inflow of USD 2.5 billion due to the deterioration in the European sovereign debt crisis; second, the interbank market experienced an inflow of USD 3 billion of RMB bond investment by nonresident RMB holders; and third, the net inflows of overseas funding of domestic enterprises and QFIIs totaled USD 3.5 billion.

For other investment, the deficit surged in the second quarter due to the increased net outflow of external loans by banks and deposits, which totaled USD 89 billion, accounting for 73 percent of the net outflow of other investment assets. In the meantime, other investment liabilities, such as trade credit and external funding, continued to post a net inflow of USD 27 billion, suggesting that external funding was accessible to domestic institutions.

Chart C3-1

Quarterly Behavior of the Major Items Under the Capital and Financial Account, from 2007 to the First Half of 2012

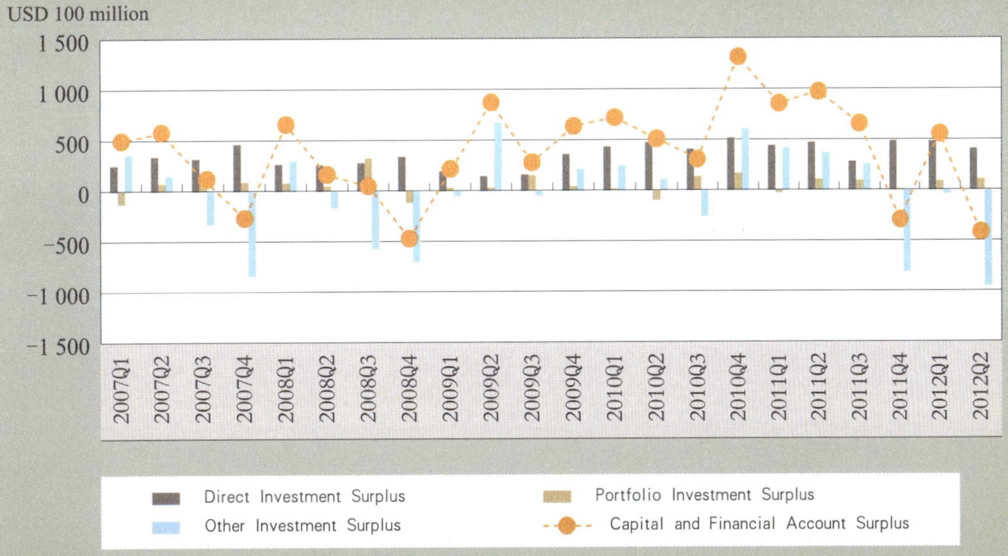

Sources: SAFE.

Ⅱ. Analysis of the Major Items in the Balance of Payments

(I) Trade in Goods

According to the statistics of the General Administration of Customs, China's trade in goods showed the following characteristics in the first half of 2012:

Foreign trade growth decelerated with a dropped foreign trade dependency. In the first half of the year, the volume of foreign trade grew by 8 percent year on year, down 18 percentage points. The ratio of exports, imports, and foreign trade to GDP was 26.5 percent, 24.6 percent, and 51.1 percent respectively, down by 1.3 percentage points, 1.8 percentage points, and 3.1 percentage points year on year (see Chart 2-1), indicating that endogeneity in the Chinese economy was further strengthened.

Chart 2-1

The Ratio of Imports to GDP and the Ratio of Exports to GDP, from 2000 to the First Half of 2012

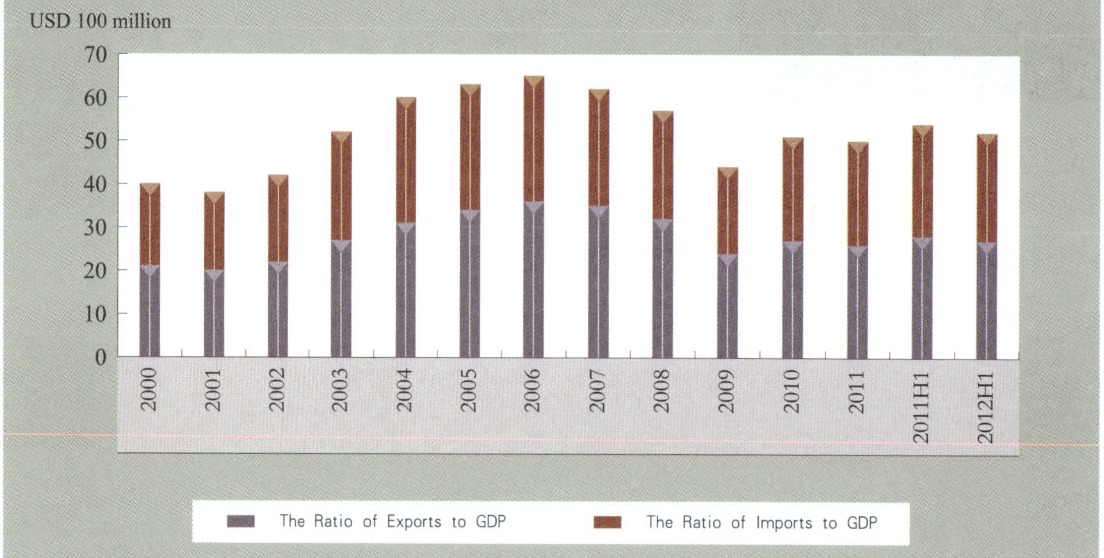

Sources: General Administration of Customs, NBS.

Exports grew more than imports and the trade surplus rebounded. In the first half of the year, exports and imports increased by 9 percent and 7 percent respectively, resulting in a total surplus of USD 68.9 billion, indicating growth of 56 percent. The ratio of the surplus to GDP was 1.9 percent, up by 0.5 percentage point (see Chart

2–2). The deceleration in import growth was driven by two major factors. One was that the drop in the growth of import prices effectively cut China's import costs. With the decrease in the price of bulk commodity, the import prices grew by a monthly average of 1.7 in the first half of the year, down 13.1 percentage points year on year, whereas the index of import volume grew by 6.4 percent monthly, which was 5.1 percentage points lower year on year (see Chart 2–3). The other factor was the slowdown in the growth of processing trade exports, which restrained the demand for related imports. In the first half of the year, processing trade exports grew by 6.4 percent, 4 percentage points lower than that of ordinary trade. Processing trade exports contributed to 0.7 percentage-point growth in processing trade imports, 7 percentage points lower than that of ordinary trade imports (see Chart 2–4).

Chart 2–2

The Trade Balance and its Ratio to GDP, from 2000 to the First Half of 2012

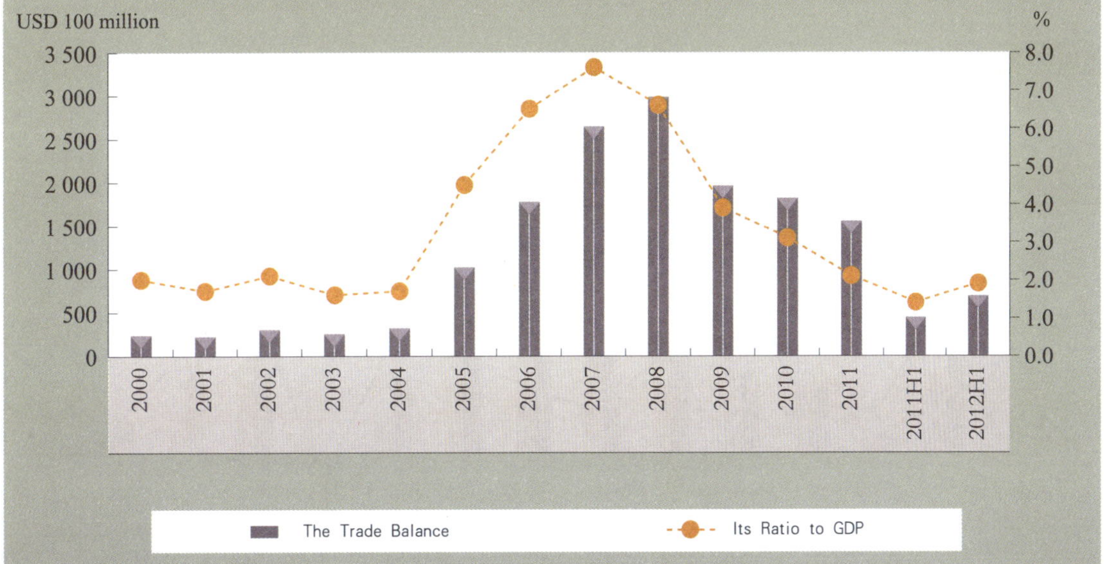

Sources: General Administration of Customs, NBS.

Chart 2-3

The Volume and Price of Trade, from January 2010 to June 2012

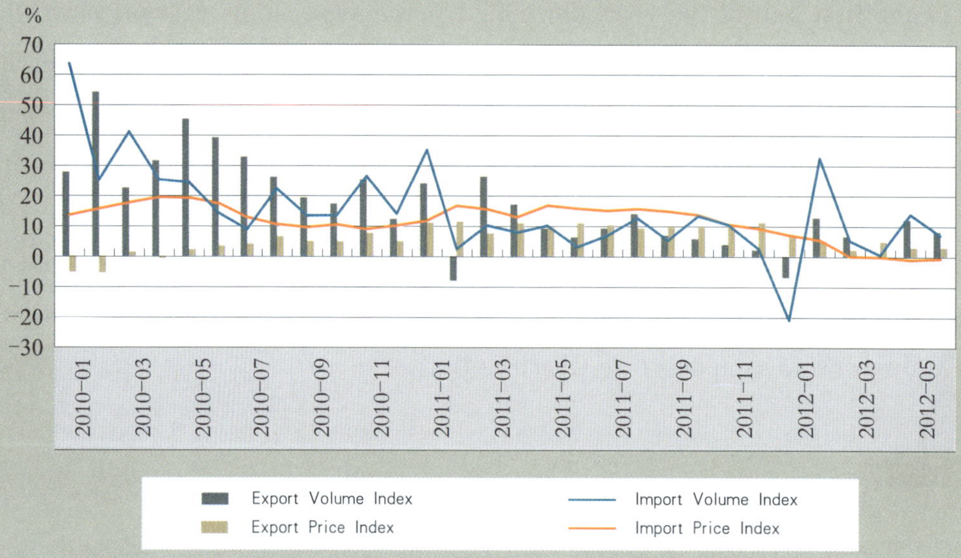

Sources: General Administration of Customs.

Chart 2-4

Patterns in the Growth Rate of Foreign Trade, from 2000 to the First Half of 2012

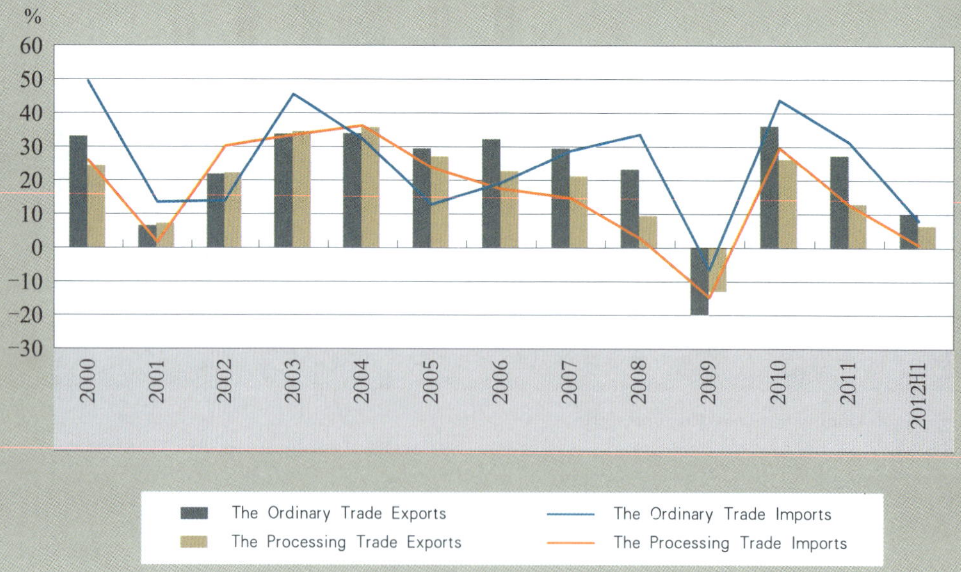

Sources: General Administration of Customs.

The processing trade surplus expanded and the ordinary trade deficit decreased. In the first half of 2012, China achieved a processing trade surplus of USD 187.4 billion, rising by 14 percent year on year. In particular, the processing trade surplus by foreign-funded enterprises amounted to USD 163.1 billion, up by 15 percent year on year and accounting for 87 percent of the total processing trade surplus, 1 percentage higher year on year. In the meantime, the ordinary trade deficit totaled USD 53.9 billion (see Chart 2–5), down by 7 percent year on year due to the rapid growth of private enterprise exports.

Chart 2–5

The Composition of the Balance of Trade in Goods, from 2000 to the First Half of 2012

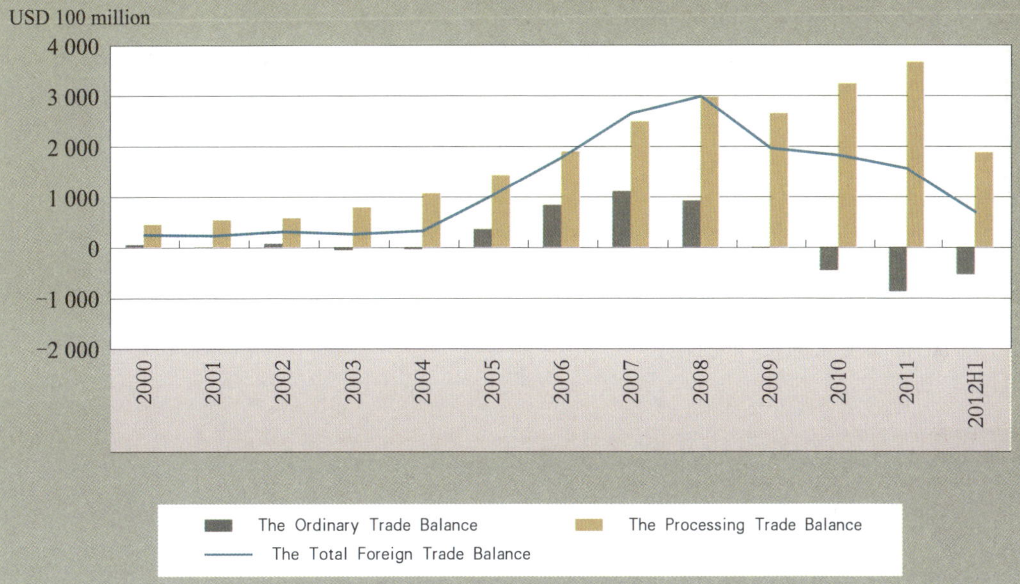

Sources: General Administration of Customs.

Foreign trade diversification was further improved, and trade with the emerging economies grew faster than trade with the advanced economies. In the first half of 2012, bilateral trade with South Africa, Russia, Brazil, and the ASEAN grew faster than total trade by 29 percentage points, 14 percentage points, 4 percentage points, and 2 percentage points respectively, accounting for a total 0.8 percentage point higher of the total trade year on year. China's trade with the EU increased by only 0.7 percent year on year, and trade with Japan decreased by 0.2 percent. The proportion of trade with the EU and Japan to the total trade dropped by 1.8

percentage points. Trade with the United States increased by 12 percent and its share was slightly enhanced.

Chart 2-6

The Growth Rate of Trade with China's Major Partners in the First Half of 2012

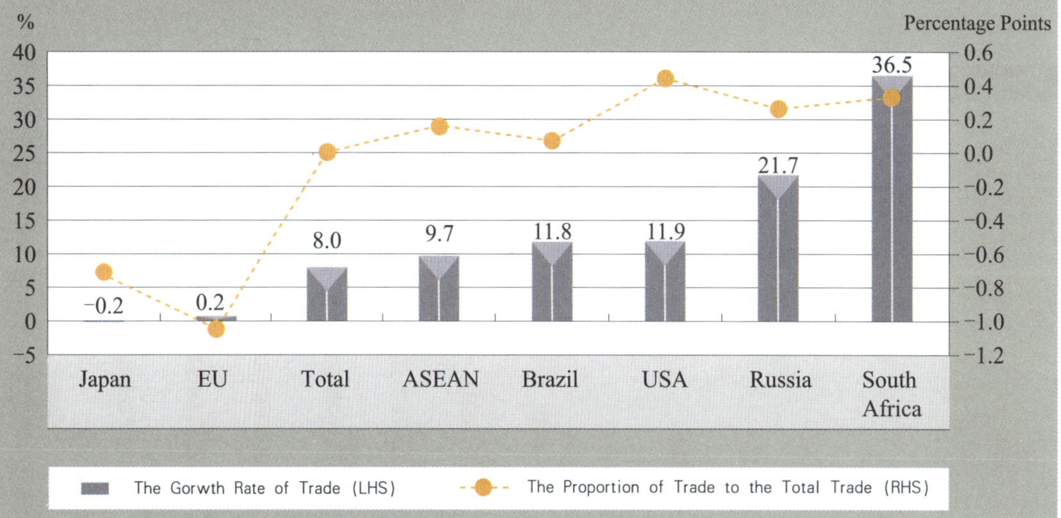

Sources: General Administration of Customs.

Box 4

An Analysis of China's Export Revenue

The export situation exerts an important influence on export revenue. According to statistics of the General Administraion of Customs, exports grew by 9 percent in the first half of 2012 year on year, which was substantially lower than the growth rate in the first half of 2011 (24 percent). As a result, growth of export revenue slowed down. BOP statistics show that export revenue increased by 8 percent year on year, far less than the growth in the first half of 2011 (29 percent).

In the first half of the year, export revenue was stable but the declining trend still should be addressed. In general, there existed a difference between goods exports and induced cross-border revenue, which was driven by two factors. One was the advanced and delayed collection of exports, which, to some extent, reflected the speed and risk of export revenue collection and is also related to the willingness of export enterprises to collect. The other factor was related to the situation of no revenue collection, seasonal fluctuations, and statistical measures, which would not change with the foreign trade environment and was relatively stable. In the first half of 2012, the ratio of cross-border revenue in trade in gwds to exports was 91 percent, remaining at a high level, and 1 percentage point lower than the ratio in the first half of 2011. However, in the second quarter, the ratio was 85 percent, significantly lower than the ratio in the first quarter and 5 percentage points lower year on year (see Chart C4–1). The decline in the ratio reflected, on the one hand, that export revenue was impacted by tightened liquidity in international markets and the deteriorating financial status of China's trading partners since the last year, and the increased risk of revenue collection. On the other hand, it indicated that under the circumstances of bi-directional RMB exchange rate fluctuations, the Willigness of holding and settlement of exchange reduced.

Chart C4–1

Quarterly Exports and Their Revenue from 2010 Q1 to 2012 Q2

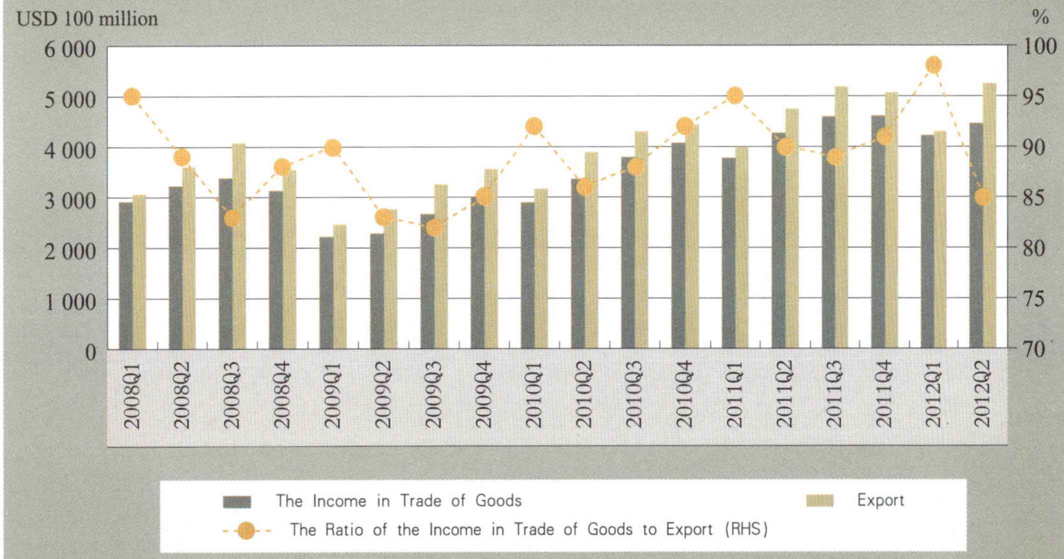

Sources: SAFE, General Administration of Customs.

In the future, we should pay attention to export revenue collection risks. Influenced by the deceleration in external economic growth, the breweing of the European sovereign debt crisis, and the fluctuating international financial markets, domestic enterprises will face export revenue collection uncertainities during specific periods and in specific regions. The State Administration of Foreign Exchange will continue to support the policy of stabilizing foreign trade growth, carry out the foreign administrative reform of trade in goods, further fulfil the measures to facilitate trade, strengthen export competitiveness, and guard against export revenue collection risks.

(II) Trade in Services

Trade in services maintained rapid growth. Based on the balance-of-payment statistics, trade in services totaled USD 220.8 billion in the first half of 2012, increasing by 10 percent year on year, which was 2 percentage points higher than that of trade in goods and accounted for 12 percent of trade in goods, almost the same level year on year (see Chart 2–7).

Chart 2–7

Trade in Goods and Trade in Services, from 2005 to the First Half of 2012

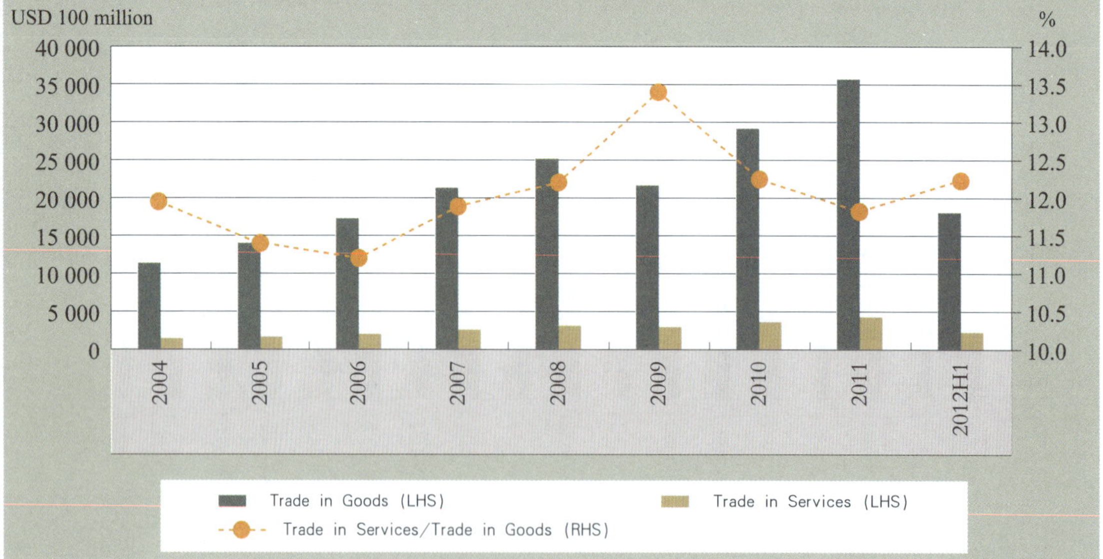

Sources: SAFE.

The large deficit in transportation and travel was the main reason for the significant surge in the trade in services deficit. In the first half of 2012, trade in services posted a deficit of USD 40.3 billion, nearly one time the growth year on year. In particular, the transportation deficit was USD 22.9 billion and the travel deficit was USD 21.8 billion, 10 percent and 1.1 times higher year on year. The transportation item maintained a large long-run deficit due to the persistent growth of foreign trade, which caused the surging demand for international cargo transportation by domestic enterprises and the growth of transportation service payments. Under the travel item, in the first half of 2012, visitors to China totaled 13.46 million, 5 percent higher year on year, driving a small growth in the travel revenue of accommodations and restaurants. Outbound visitors totaled 38.56 million, up by 20 percent, and travel payments, shopping, and study grew substantially. In terms of countries and regions, the travel deficits to the United States, Australia, and the Hong Kong SAR were high (see Chart 2–8) in the first half of 2012 mainly due to rapid increase in study expenditures in the above three countries and regions.

Chart 2–8

The Composition of Countries and Regions Under the Travel Item, in the First Half of 2012

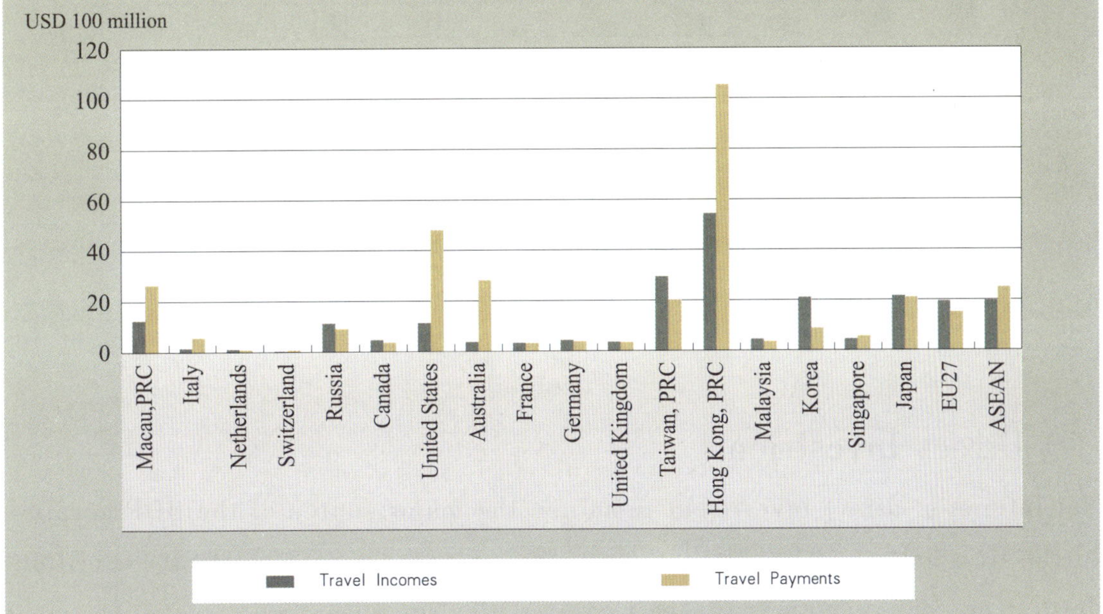

Sources: SAFE.

Partners for trade in services were highly concentrated. Major trading partners were neighboring countries and developed countries in Europe and the United States; the top ten trading partners accounted for 73 percent of the total trade in services (see Chart 2-9). In particular, trade with Hong Kong SAR recorded a surplus of USD 18 billion, and trade with other main trading partners posted a deficit. The major deficit partners included Australia, the United States, and Korea, with deficits of USD 5.9 billion, USD 5.6 billion, and USD 5.2 billion respectively.

Chart 2-9

The Composition of Countries and Regions Under the Service Trade Item, in the First Half of 2012

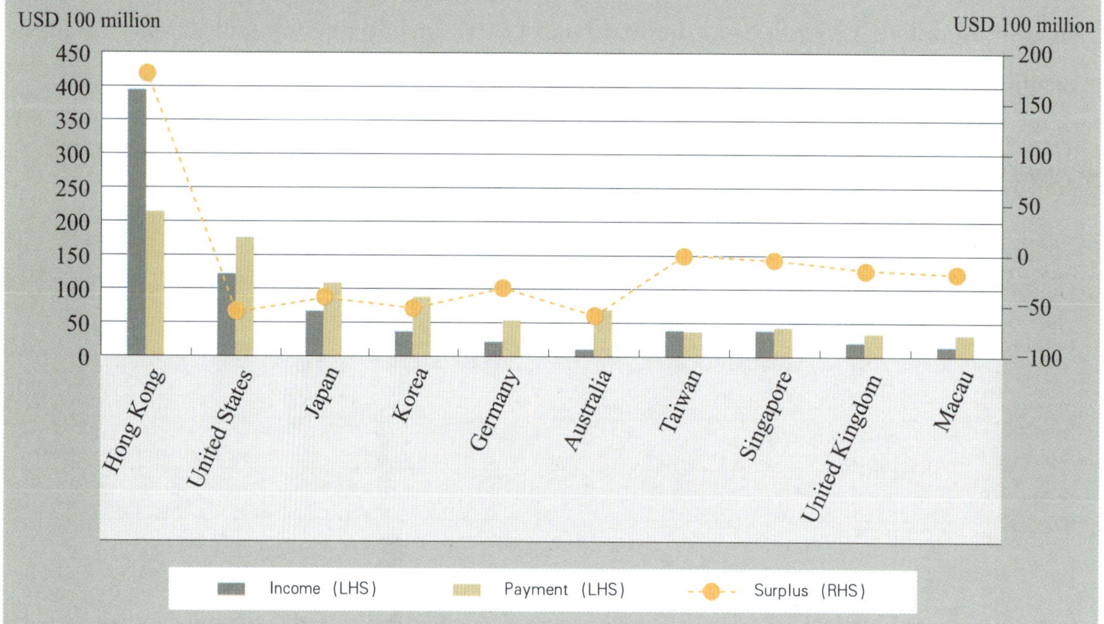

Sources: SAFE.

(Ⅲ) Direct Investment

Net inflows of direct investment remained the major source of the BOP surplus. In the first half of 2012, direct investment posted a surplus of USD 90 billion, down 3 percent year on year (see Chart 2-10). Net inflows of direct investment accounted for 98 percent of the total BOP surplus, 64 percentage points higher year on year, which, on the one hand, indicated that direct investment helped stabilize the BOP situation, and, on the other, showed China's status as a major global direct investment host country because of its steady economic growth against the background of international turbulence.

Chart 2-10

The Surplus in Direct Investment, from 2000 to the First Half of 2012

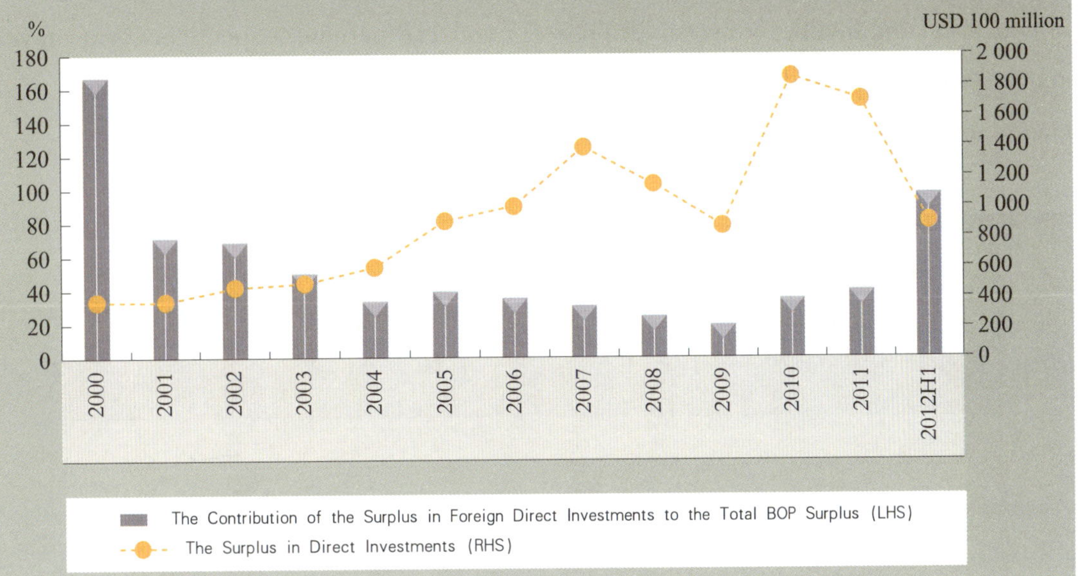

Sources: SAFE.

Foreign direct investment experienced a slightly increased inflow as well as a net inflow. In the first half of 2012, inward foreign direct investment inflows and outflows amounted to USD 131.4 billion and USD 13.3 billion respectively, growing by 7 percent and 15 percent year on year. The major reason for the increased outflow was the accelerated external debt payments to foreign shareholders by foreign-funded enterprises, which increased by 50 percent in the first half of the year. The withdrawal of inward FDI decreased by 8 percent year on year. Because inward FDI inflows were much higher than FDI outflows, inward FDI recorded a net inflow of USD 118.1 billion, increasing USD 7 billion and 6 percent year on year, maintaining the increasing trend and the decreasing growth rate since the first half of 2009 (see Chart 2-11).

The composition of inward FDI improved further. Investment from the major advanced countries continued to increase. In the first half of 2012, inward FDI from France,

Germany, Japan, and the United States in the nonbanking sectors increased by 110 percent, 96 percent, 29 percent, and 20 percent respectively. Inward FDI from offshore centers decreased. Inward FDI from the Cayman Islands, the British Virgin Islands, and Hong Kong SAR dropped by 37 percent, 35 percent, and 15 percent respectively. In terms of industries, manufacturing, real estate, leasing and business services, wholesale and retail services, and mining continued to be the major inward FDI industries. Inward FDI in education and health increased 200 percent and 110 percent respectively year on year, and inward FDI in real estate dropped by 25 percent, reflecting an active effect of the macro policy on real estate.

Chart 2-11

Inward FDI, from 2000 to the First Half of 2012

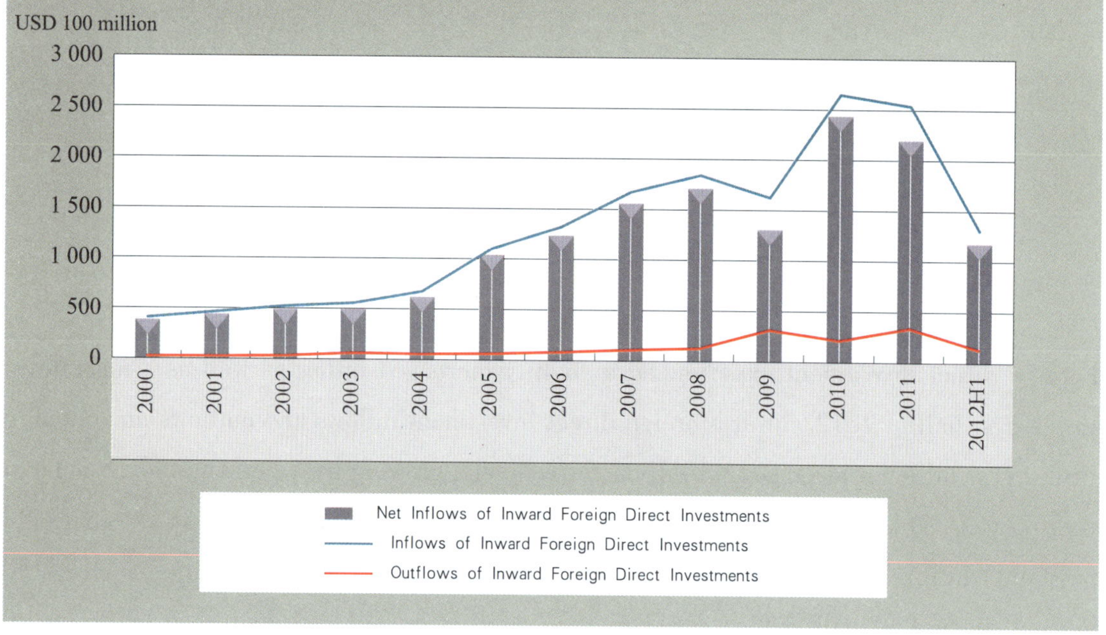

Sources: SAFE.

Outflows and net outflows of outward direct investment grew substantially. In the first half of 2012, outflows of outward direct investment increased 45 percent to USD 38 billion; withdrawals of outward direct investment increased 25 percent to USD 10 billion. As a result, net outflows of outward direct investment totaled USD 28.1 billion, up by 53 percent (see Chart 2-12).

Chart 2–12

Outflows and Net Outflows of Outward Direct Investment, from 2000 to the First Half of 2012

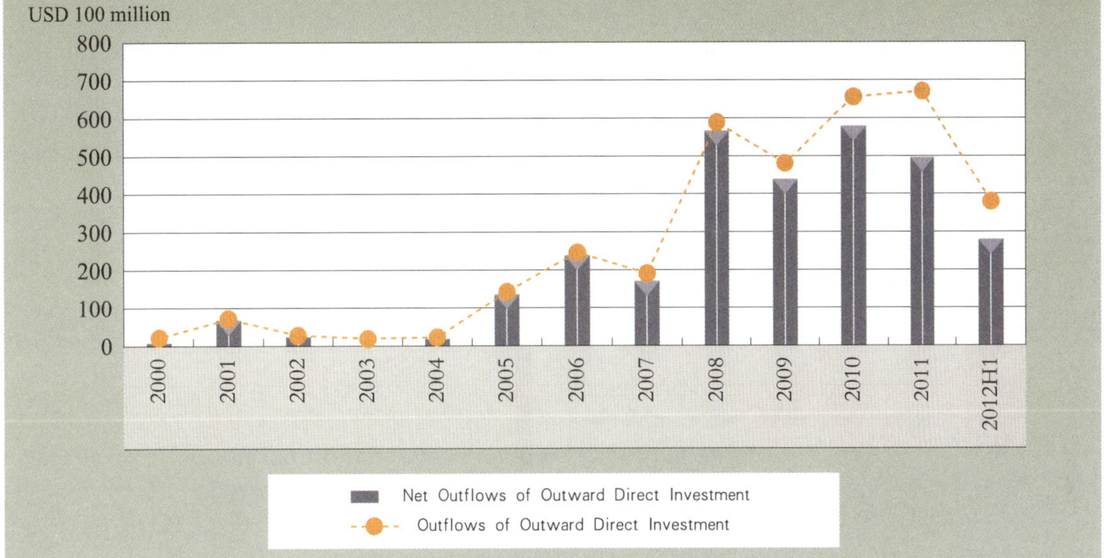

Sources: SAFE.

(Ⅳ) Portfolio Investment

Portfolio investment maintained a surplus. In the first half of 2012, portfolio investment recorded a net inflow of USD 20.4 billion, a 1.4-fold increase year on year. In particular, outbound portfolio investment posted a net inflow of USD 5.9 billion, a 9.9-fold increase; and inbound portfolio investment achieved a net inflow of USD 14.5 billion, up by 84 percent year on year (see Chart 2–13).

Outbound portfolio investment retreated markedly. In the first half of 2012, the recovery of the global economy slowed down, the European sovereign debt crisis deteriorated, and turbulence in international financial markets intensified, which together led to more cautious outbound portfolio investment. Outflows of outbound portfolio investment amounted to USD 8.5 billion, down by 23 percent; and inflows totaled USD 14.3 billion, up by 24 percent year on year. In particular, both the outflows and inflows of outbound equity portfolio investment decreased and net inflows totaled USD 2.2 billion. Inflows of outbound debt portfolio investment grew by 1 fold and recorded a net inflow of USD 3.6 billion, which posted a net outflow of USD 200 million at the same time last year. In the first half of 2012, outbound portfolio investment by QDII fluctuated: the first quarter experienced a net inflow of USD 500 million but in the second quarter a net outflow of USD 600 million, and net increase reached USD 100 million.

Chart 2-13

Net Flows of Portfolio Investment, from 2000 to the First Half of 2012

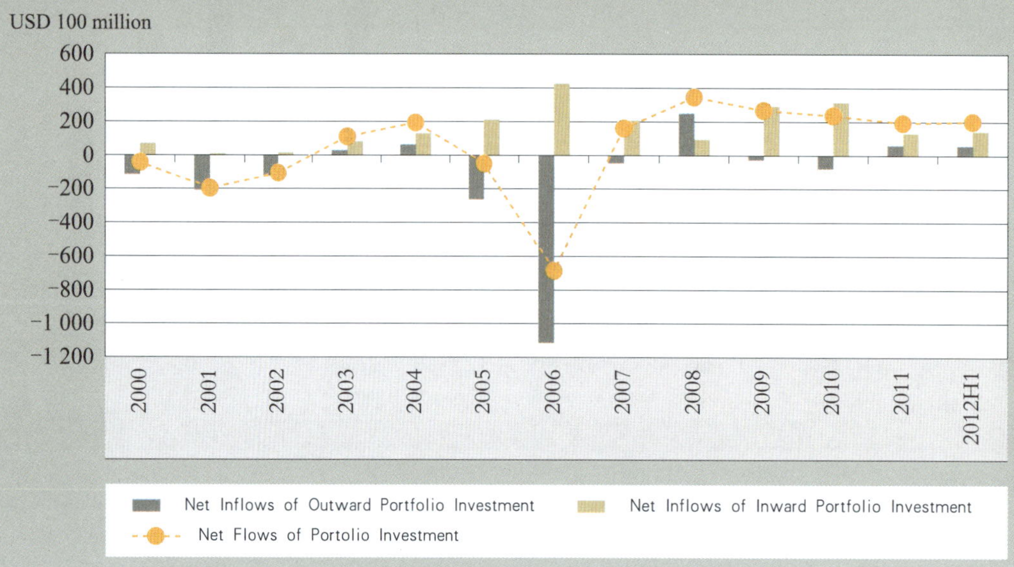

Notes: Positive outward portfolio investment refer to net inflows, otherwise net outflows. Positive inward portfolio investments refer to net inflows, otherwise net outflows.

Sources: SAFE.

Inbound portfolio investment were active. In the first half of 2012, inflows of inbound portfolio investment totaled USD 16.6 billion and outflows totaled 2.1 billion, up by 86 percent and 95 percent respectively. In terms of their composition, inbound debt portfolio investment became more attractive since domestic inflation was dropping and there were strong expectations of a cut in interest rates. In the first half of 2012, the three categories of institutions that are allowed to invest in the domestic interbank bond market, including overseas RMB settlement banks, made active investment in the interbank bond market. Moreover, the Ministry of Finance and domestic institutions also issued RMB bonds in the Hong Kong market. As a result, inbound debt portfolio investment posted a net inflow of USD 9.2 billion, whereas there had been a net outflow in the first half of 2011. In terms of equity portfolio investment, impacted by expectations of decreased earnings of domestic enterprises and the downturn in international capital markets, inbound equity portfolio investment recorded an inflow of USD

7.4 billion and an outflow of USD 2.1 billion respectively, down by 17 percent and up by 96 percent. Net inflows totaled USD 5.3 billion, 33 percent lower year on year. In particular, domestic enterprises raised USD 3.9 billion by public offerings abroad, down by 35 percent year on year. Inbound portfolio investment by QFII grew steadily, which in the first quarter recorded nearly equal inflows and outflows, and in the second quarter recorded net inflows of USD 1.5 billion and the first half of the year recorded net inflows of USD 1.6 billion.

(V) Trade Credit

Trade credit① increased in terms of assets and liabilities. By the end of June, outstanding trade credit assets totaled USD 310.1 billion, representing growth of USD 33.2 billion and 12 percent from the end of 2011. Outstanding trade credit liabilities totaled USD 290.1 billion, up by USD 40.9 billion and 16 percent from the end of 2011. Trade credit posted net assets of USD 20 billion, USD 7.7 billion less than that at the end of 2011 and a decrease of 28 percent. By the end of June, trade credit assets and liabilities accounted for 8.2 percent and 7.7 percent respectively of the total foreign trade in the past 12 months, up by 0.6 percentage point and 0.8 percentage point from the end of 2011 (see Chart 2–14)

Trade credit recorded a net inflow with fluctuations. In the first half of 2012, the net inflow of trade credit was USD 7.7 billion. In particular, net assets of trade credit dropped by USD 22.3 billion due significantly to increased liabilities and decreased assets in the first quarter, which meant a net inflow; but in the second quarter net assets of trade credit rose substantially by USD 14.7 billion due to rising assets and dropping liabilities, which meant a net outflow.

Trade credit for both exports and imports increased. By the end of June 2012, export collectables totaled USD 256.6 billion, up by 17 percent from the end of 2011; and export advance collections totaled USD 58.9 billion, up by 2 percent. Export collectables exceeded export advance collections by USD 197.7 billion. Import advance payments amounted to USD 53.6 billion, down by 7 percent from the end of 2011; import payables amounted to USD 231.2 billion, up by 21

① Trade credit refers to payables and collectables of domestic enterprises with nonresidents due to trade transactions. The asset side includes collectables and advance payments, and the liability side includes payables and advance collections. Trade credit reflects an entity's position with its trading partner, excluding trade financing and financing guarantees from banks. Trade credit assets and liabilities are important components under the item of other investments of the capital and financial account of the BOP. In addition, trade credit liability is a very important source of data on China's external debt statistics. The sum of the outstanding trade credit and the outstanding registered external debt is the total external debt.

percent. Import payables exceeded import advance payments by USD 177.6 billion.

Chart 2-14

Outstanding Trade Credit Assets and Liabilities, from 2005 to the End of June 2012

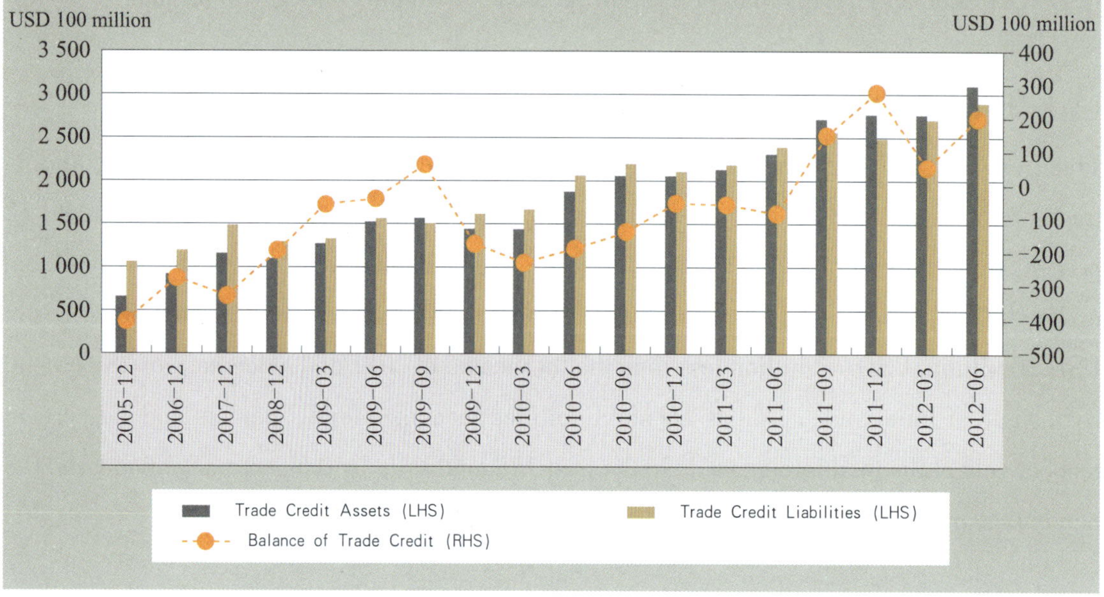

Sources: SAFE.

Trade credit tended to be short in terms of maturity. For sample enterprises, by the end of June 2012, trade credit assets with a maturity of less than one year accounted for 95 percent of total trade credit assets, 5 percentage points higher than that at the end of 2011; and trade credit liabilities with a maturity of less than one year accounted for 94 percent of total trade credit liabilities, 1 percentage point higher than that at the end of 2011.

Foreign-funded enterprises played a more active role than Chinese-funded enterprises in terms of trade credit. By the end of June 2012, sample foreign-funded enterprises held 57 percent of their total external assets as trade credit assets, and 53 percent of the total external liabilities as trade credit liabilities. Foreign-funded enterprises were more inclined to make capital arrangements by collectables and payables. Collectables and payables by foreign-funded enterprises accounted for 62 percent of the total. However, Chinese-funded enterprises preferred advance collections and advance payments for capital arrangements, which accounted for 75 percent of the total.

Ⅲ. Operations of the Foreign Exchange Market and the RMB Exchange Rate

(I) Reform and Development of the Foreign Exchange Market

Management of the comprehensive foreign exchange positions of purchases and sales for banks was improved. In order to be consistent with the reform on April 16, which enlarged the floating band of the RMB exchange rate against the USD and increased the RMB exchange rate elasticity, we canceled the temporary management that had required lower limits to the real receipt and payment positions for banks since November 2010, and we began to implement positive and minus band management for the comprehensive foreign exchange positions of purchases and sales for banks. The banks had more flexibility and initiative to carry out foreign exchange transactions and to implement risk management, which helped to form the RMB exchange rate.

The coverage for squaring the exposure of precious metals to the exchange rate by banks was broadened. Policies for squaring the exposure of gold to the exchange rate began to apply to silver, platinum, and other precious metals, so banks could offer customers more investment choices, which is a way to support individuals to hold more precious metals.

Participation by small and medium-sized financial institutions in the foreign exchange market was facilitated. We reduced or exempted the transaction fees for rural banks when they entered the foreign exchange market in an attempt to support the agricultural industry through foreign exchange policies. We simplified management for entry into the interbank foreign exchange and currency swap markets. We added more ways to exchange the principals of foreign currency swaps. As a result, the financial sector could better serve the real economy.

The pilot program for RMB and foreign currency conversion franchises of individuals was expanded. By simplifying entry management, encouraging branded chains, and strengthening risk control, we developed a regulated, effective, and diversified market system for RMB and foreign currency conversion by individuals whereby the banks play the main role and the franchise institutions play a complementary role.

(II) Trends in the RMB Exchange Rate

The RMB exchange rate showed enhanced two-way fluctuations. At the end of June 2012, the mid-price for the RMB against the USD was 6.3249, a depreciation of 0.4 percent from the end of 2011 (see Chart 3-1) and an appreciation of 30.9 percent from the reform of the regime in 2005. In the 117 trading days in the first half of 2012, the daily average fluctuation of the mid-price of the RMB against the USD reached 55 bps (43 bps in 2011), with 56 appreciations and 61 depreciations, a more obvious indication that the exchange rate was referring to the currency basket. In the first half of 2012, the RMB appreciated by 3.7 percent against the Euro and 1.8 percent against the JNY.

Chart 3-1

Trends in the RMB Exchange Rate against the USD, Euro, and JPY, in the First Half of 2012

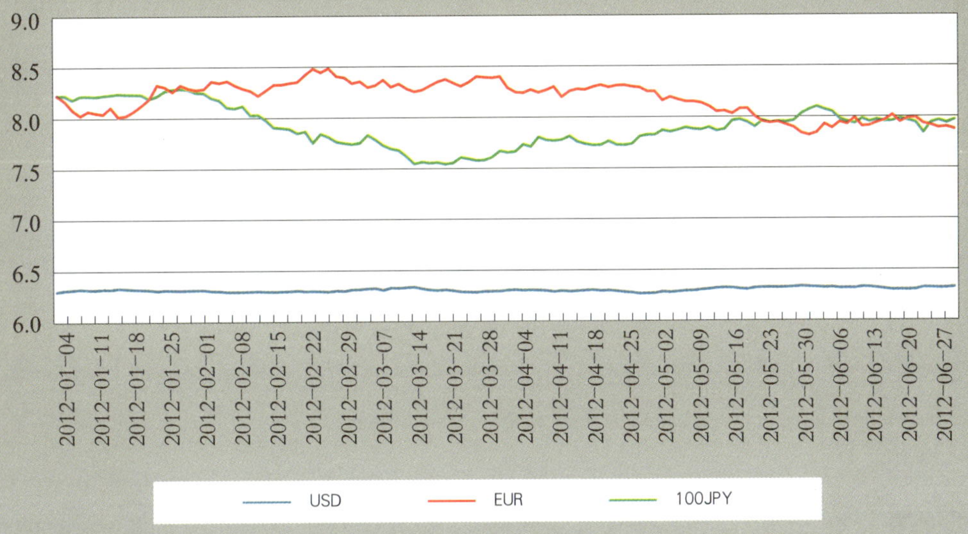

Sources: CFETS.

The RMB exchange rate maintained a reasonable and balanced level. In the first half of 2012, the largest daily fluctuation of the spot RMB/USD trading price against the mid-price in the interbank market reached 0.34 percent, higher than the 0.18 percent in 2011. After April 16 when the daily floating band of the RMB was enlarged, it increased further to 0.53 percent and the highest level even touched the upper limit of the 1 percent floating band (see Chart 3-2). After that the People's Bank of China intervened much less in the foreign exchange market, the autonomous system became steadier so that market supply and demand could decide the exchange rate and the exchange rate could also adjust market supply and demand. In the first half of 2012, both the domestic and overseas forward RMB/USD exchange rates showed two-way movements (see Chart 3-3). At the end of June 2012, the domestic interbank forward price, the NDF, and the one-year deliverable forward price in Hong Kong saw the RMB depreciating by 1.2 percent, 1.4 percent, and 1.9 percent respectively, far lower than the 7 percent during the 2008 international financial crisis.

It reflected the interest rate spread between the tight RMB and the loose USD. The depreciation was not only about exchange rate expectations, and it also meant that the RMB was at a reasonable level which was accepted by the market and it did not face big depreciation pressure.

Chart 3-2

Fluctuations of the Spot RMB Exchange Rate against the USD in the Interbank Foreign Exchange Market, in the First Half of 2012

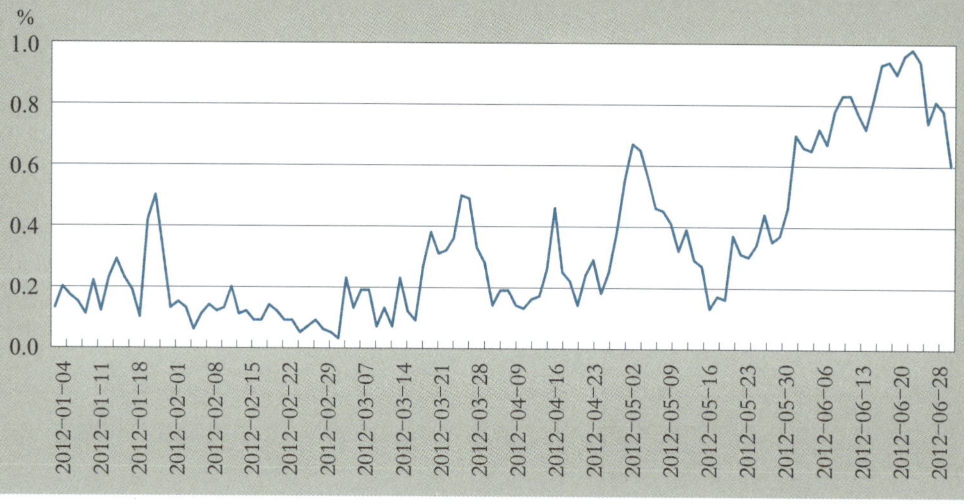

Note: The largest fluctuation in the daily trading price against the mid-price.

Sources: CFETS.

Chart 3-3

One-Year RMB Appreciation and Depreciation Expectations against the USD in the Domestic and Overseas Markets, in the First Half of 2012

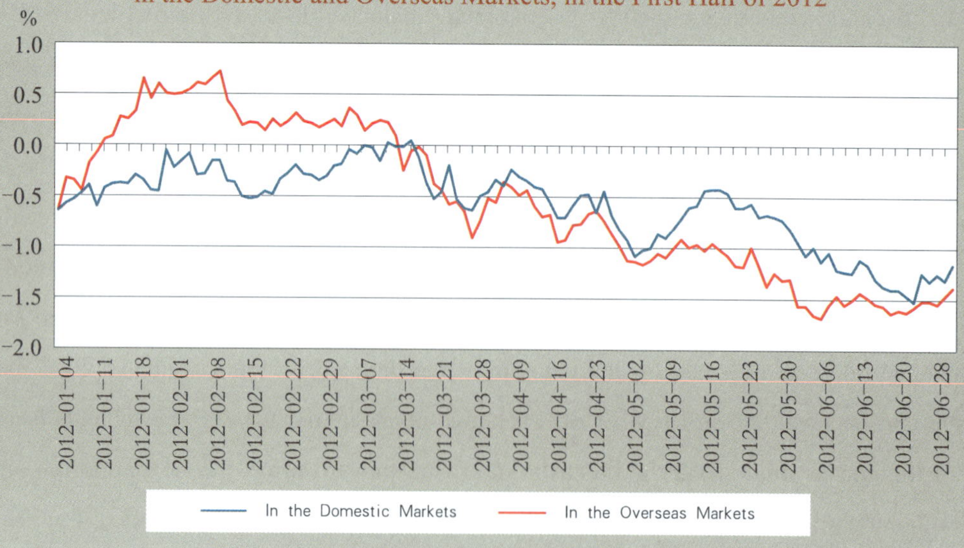

Sources: CFETS, Reuters.

The RMB effective exchange rate appreciated. According to the BIS, in the first half of 2012 the nominal effective exchange rate of the RMB appreciated by 1.6 percent against the currency basket. Deducting for inflation, the real effective exchange rate of the RMB appreciated by 0.9 percent. Among the 61 currencies observed by the BIS, the RMB ranked 16th in terms of the extent of appreciation of the nominal effective exchange rate and ranked 22nd in terms of the extent of appreciation of the real effective exchange rate, indicating that the RMB was performing steadily among the currencies of the emerging economies. The nominal and real effective exchange rates of the RMB appreciated by 23.1 percent and 30.4 percent respectively from the regime reform in 2005 (see Chart 3-4).

Chart 3-4

Trends in the RMB Effective Exchange Rate, from 1994 to the First Half of 2012

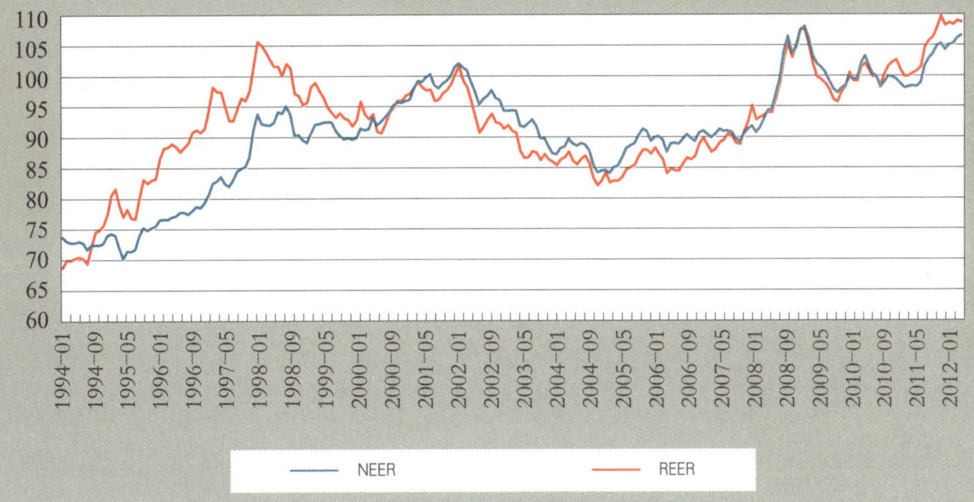

Sources:BIS.

Box 5

Comparison of China's Balance-of-payments Condition with That of the Other BRIC Countries

When measuring cross-border capital flows, the international method mainly uses the data in the capital and financial account of the balance of payments (not including changes in reserve assets), which cover foreign direct investment, portfolio investment, and other investment. From 2005 to 2011, net capital inflows of China, India, and Brazil reached USD 0.96 trillion, 0.39 trillion, and 0.40 trillion respectively, and Russia experienced net capital outflows of USD 0.17 trillion (see Chart C5–1). When analyzing the details for the BRIC countries, we find different "features."

Table C5–1 Capital Account Conditions in the BRIC Countries from 2005 to 2011

Unit: USD 100 millions

	Foreign Direct Investment	Outward Direct Investment	Foreign Portfolio Investment	Outward Portfolio Investment	Foreign Other Investment	Outward Other Investment
China	11 509	−2 631	1 696	−1 207	6 140	−5 936
	8 878		489		204	
India	2 001	−1 017	1 142	-14	1 300	−41
	984		1 128		1 753	
Russia	3 053	−3 009	−576	25	3 014	−4 209
	44		−551		−1 195	
Brazil	2 546	−587	1 924	187	1 439	−1 492
	1 959		2 111		−53	

Note: A positive value represents capital inflows, a negative value represents capital outflows.

Sources: SAFE, The Central Bank of Russia, CEIC.

China's capital inflow channels were very steady. As the most important channel of capital inflows for the BRIC countries, FDI is especially important to China. In terms of the amount of the flow, from 2005 to 2011 China's cumulative net FDI reached USD 1.15 trillion, 120 percent of the net capital inflows during the same period and exceeding the total amount of India, Russia, and Brazil. Cumulative net foreign portfolio investment reached USD 169.6 billion, accounting for only 18 percent of the net capital inflows during the same period, whereas in India the percentage was 31 percent and in Brazil it was 47 percent. In terms of the outstanding amount, by the end of 2011, FDI accounted for 61 percent of China's total external liabilities, obviously higher than that of India, Russia, and Brazil, at 32 percent, 41 percent, and 44 percent respectively. Portfolio investment only accounted for 8 percent, far lower than that of India, Russia, and Brazil, at 24 percent, 21 percent, and 44 percent respectively. The relatively steady FDI dominated cross-border capital inflows. It meant that even if the external environment was to become worse and foreign portfolio investment, which are sensitive to risks and quite volatile, were withdrawn, their impact would be less on China than on the other emerging markets.

International banks had small net exposures to China. In recent years, we had both capital inflows and outflows in cross-border commercial and banking credits (they are recorded under the item of other investment as trade credits, loans, and deposits in the balance of payments), with cumulative net inflows standing at USD 34.7 billion. The figures for India, Russia, and Brazil were USD 175.3 billion, USD 70.5 billion, and USD 14.3 billion respectively. At the end of 2011, China's net external liabilities under the item of cross-border commercial and banking credit reached USD 86.3 billion, while they were USD 269.7 billion for India, USD 112.6 billion for Russia, and USD 59.6 billion for Brazil. According to the BIS, by the end of 2011 claims by European and US banks to China accounted for 70.1 percent of the total claims to China by international banks, lower than that of India, Russia, and Brazil, at 73.1 percent, 94.9 percent, and 93.3 percent respectively. With respect to domestic debt, banks are the main source for financing (the percentages for China, India, Russia, and Brazil were 47.2 percent, 27.3 percent, 26.6 percent, and 14.4 percent respectively). Direct funding by corporations was relatively small. This meant that the deleveraging process in the European and US banking sectors had a smaller impact on China than it had on other countries. The real economy was buffered from the banking sector.

China's trade conditions are better than those of the other BRIC countries. Trade conditions are an important indicator measuring a country's external payments and long-term solvency. For those countries that depend on capital inlows to meet their savings gap, if inflows cannot effectively improve their international competiveness and trade conditions, it may hurt their solvency or even cause the withdrawl of debt capital. Actually, the combination of trade deficits and short-term capital inflows is recognized as a sign of a currency or financial crisis. One example is that of Thailand during the 1997 Asian financial crisis. In India, the non-oil trade deficit continued for 8 years and the degree of maturity of its exports was under the average level in Asia. Trade in Russia and Brazil mainly depend on bulk commodity exports. In contrast, China has obvious advantages in trade, such as the reform and opening policies, the steady commercial environment, and the integrated manufacturing chains. These advantages that have developed over the past 10 years will not disappear in the short term nor will they move abroad on a large scale.

The balance-of-payments conditions in recent years show that China's cross-border capital flows reflect conditions in the real economy and are resistent to external shocks, which helps to avoid a large fluctuation in the RMB exchange rate. In the first half of 2012, the nominal effective exchange rate of the RMB appreciated by 1.6 percent against the currency basket, while there was an depreciation of 8.4 percent in Brazil, 4.7 percent in India, 1.3 percent in Russia, and a apprieciation of 0.1 percent in South Africa.

(Ⅲ) Transactions in the Foreign Exchange Market

In the first half of 2012, the cumulative trading volume of the RMB/foreign currency market totaled USD 4.48 trillion, with a daily average trading volume of USD 38.3 billion. The daily average trading volume went up by 8.2 percent from the previous year. The total trading volume of the client market and the interbank market was USD1.55 trillion and USD 2.93 trillion respectively[①] (see Table 3-1).

Foreign exchange spot transactions grew steadily. In the first half of 2012, foreign exchange spot transactions reached USD 1.36 trillion (implementation of forwards is not included) in the client market, up 5.1 percent from 2011. Cumulative foreign exchange spot transactions in the interbank market totaled USD1.73 trillion, with a daily average trading volume of USD 14.8 billion, up 1.3 percent from 2011. In the first half of 2012, spot transactions accounted for 68.8 percent of the total transactions in the foreign exchange market, the lowest share in history (see Chart 3-5). This shows a stronger demand for foreign exchange derivatives in the market as the RMB exchange rate had more elasticity.

Foreign exchange forward transactions went down. In the first half of 2012, cumulative foreign exchange forward transactions in the client market reached USD 173.1 billion, purchases and sales of which stood at USD 83.9 billion and 89.2 billion respectively. Cumulative daily average foreign exchange forward transactions, purchases of foreign exchange, and sales of foreign exchange went down by 6.7 percent, 8.5 percent, and 5 percent from 2011, a sign that enterprises were moving from net purchases to net sales of foreign exchange (see Chart 3-6). Cumulative foreign exchange forward transactions in the interbank market totaled USD 64.5 billion, with a daily average trading volume of USD 550 million, down 37.3 percent from 2011. After that we canceled the lower limit management on the foreign exchange position of banks

① In the client market, the trading volume was calculated as the total purchases and sales of foreign exchange by clients, the interbank market only took the data for one side. The same below.

under the principle of real receipts and payments in April, the banks returned to the method of combining spot and swap transactions to cover the exposures. As a result, the demand for forwards by banks declined.

Chart 3-5

The Percentage of Spot Transactions Among Total Transactions in the Foreign Exchange Market, from 2006 to the First Half of 2012

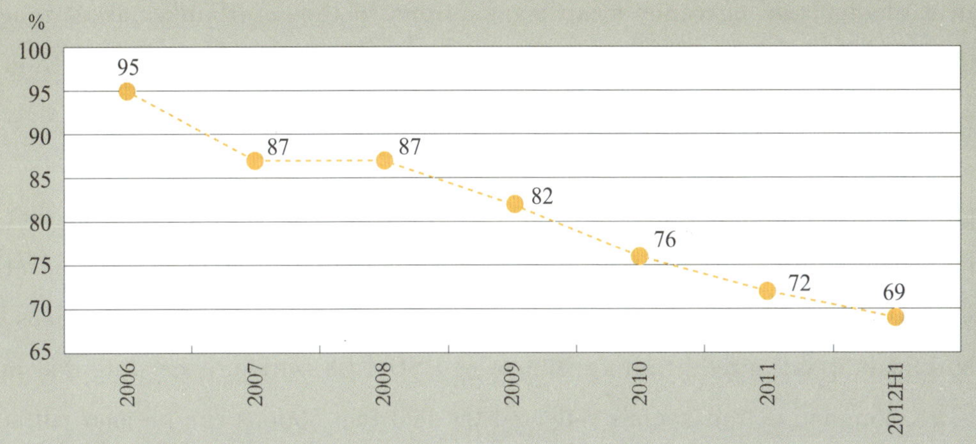

Sources: SAFE, CFETS

Chart 3-6

The Trading Volume of Forwards in the Client Market, from 2006 to the First Half of 2012

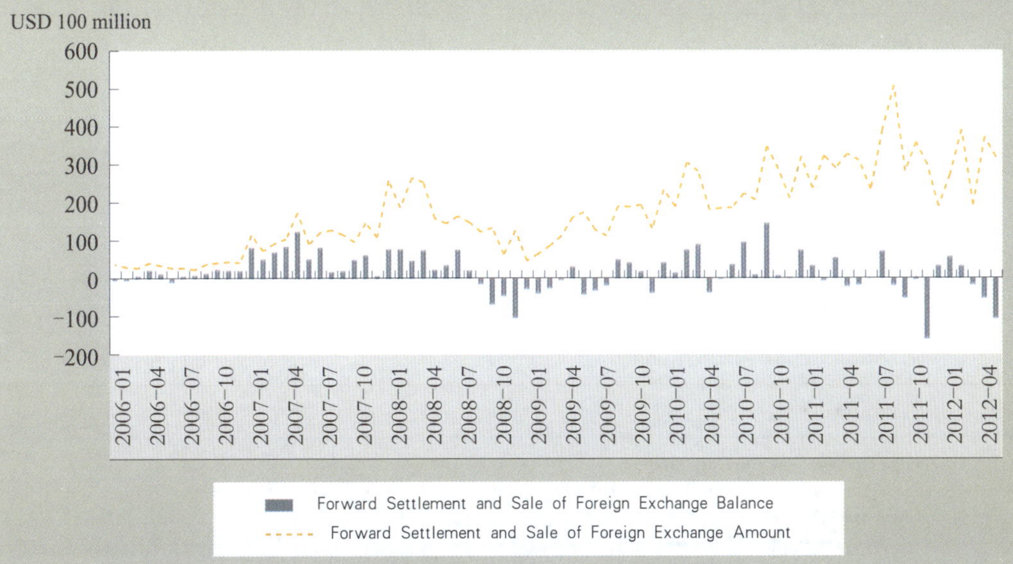

Sources: SAFE.

Foreign exchange and currency swap transactions increased greatly. In the first half of 2012, cumulative foreign exchange and currency swap transactions in the client market reached USD 15.6 billion, 1.3 times the amount in the 2011. The spot purchases/ forward sales and spot sales/forward purchases accounted for 6.3 percent and 93.7 percent respectively of the cumulative foreign exchange and currency swap transactions in the client market. This reflected the fact that through swaps, enterprises were changing RMB capital into foreign exchange capital. Cumulative foreign exchange and currency swap transactions in the interbank market reached USD 1.14 trillion. The daily average trading volume stood at USD 9.72 billion, up 33.9 percent from 2011.

Foreign exchange options grew greatly. In the first half of 2012, the client market saw a total trading volume of USD 5.91 billion, 6.8 times that in 2011. The transactions mainly focused on zero cost option portfolios, with relatively few simple call options. The interbank market saw a total trading volume of USD 1.08 billion, exceeding that in the 2011. The more active transactions reflected the fact that options can be more attractive than forwards when we manage foreign exchange risks more flexibly.

Table 3-1 Transactions in the RMB/ Foreign Exchange Market, in the First Half of 2012

Unit: USD 100 million

Products	Trading Volume
Spot	**30 861**
Client Market	13 603
Inter-Bank Foreign Exchange Market	17 258
Forward	**2 376**
Client Market	1 731
Inter-Bank Foreign Exchange Market	645
Less than 3 months (including 3 months)	387
3 months to 1 year (including 1 year)	153
More than 1 year	106
Foreign Exchange and Currency Swaps	**11 528**
Client Market	156
Inter-Bank Foreign Exchange Market	11 372

(Continued)

Products	Trading Volume
Less than 3 months (including 3 months)	10 156
3 months to 1 year (including 1 year)	1 188
More than 1 year	28
Option	**69.9**
Client Market	59.1
Foreign Exchange Call Option /RMB Put Option	29.1
Foreign Exchange Put Option /RMB Call Option	30
Inter-Bank Foreign Exchange Market	10.8
Foreign Exchange Call Option /RMB Put Option	5.8
Foreign Exchange Put Option /RMB Call Option	5.1
Less than 3 months (including 3 months)	7.9
3 months to 1 year (including 1 year)	2.9
More than 1 year	0
Total	**44 835**
Client Market	15 549
Inter-Bank Foreign Exchange Market	29 286
Spot	30 861
Forward	2 376
Foreign Exchange and Currency Swaps	11 528
Option	69.9

Note: The trading volumes here are unilateral transactions and the data use rounded numbers.

Sources: SAFE, CFETS.

The currency pairs shrank slightly. In the first half of 2012, the nine currency pairs saw a total trading volume of USD 42.8 billion, with a daily average trading volume of USD 370 million, down 5.7 percent from 2011. The spot transactions, which contributed the most to the total transactions, saw a total trading volume of USD 36.2 billion, with a daily average trading volume of USD 310 million, down 11.9 percent from 2011. In terms of trading currencies, the USD/HKD and the EURO/USD pairs dominated the market (see Chart 3–7), which was in line with the structure of international foreign exchange markets and reflected economic relations between Mainland China and Hong Kong.

Chart 3-7

The Structure of Currency Pairs in the Interbank Foreign Exchange Spot Market, from 2005 to the First Half of 2012

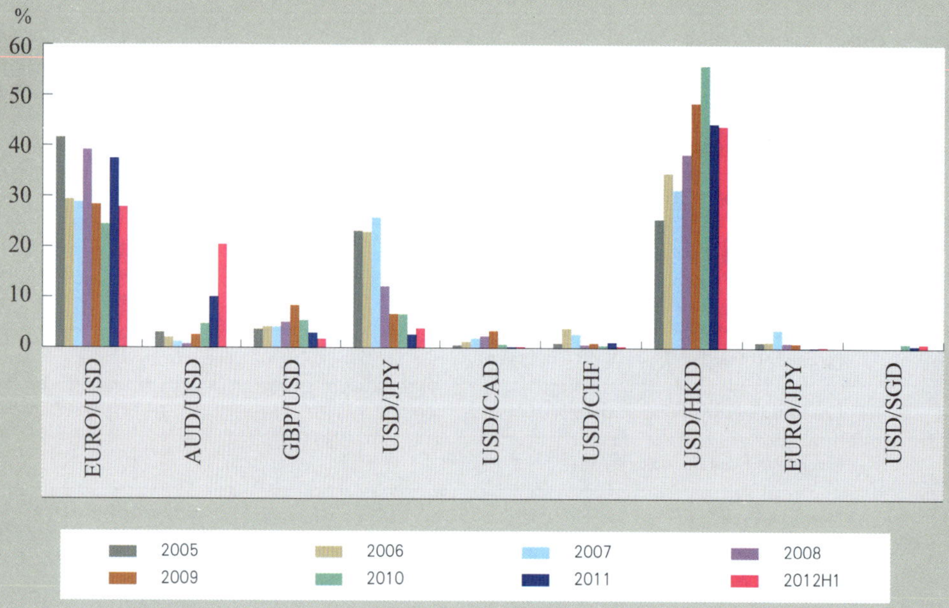

Sources: SAFE, CFETS.

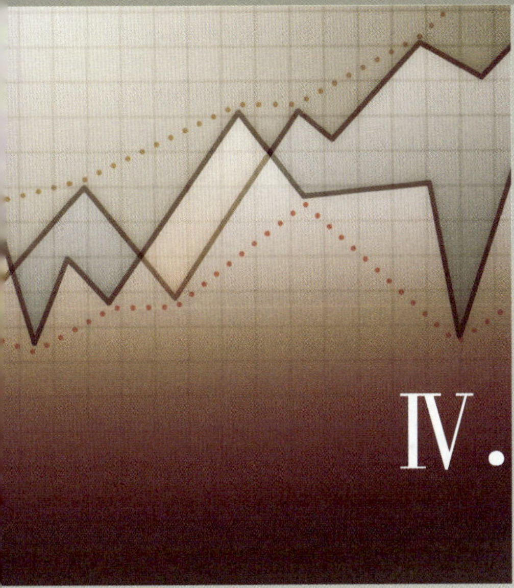

Ⅳ. BOP Outlook and Policy Orientation

Currently, the decrease in China's BOP surplus and the slowdown in the accumulation of foreign exchange reserves accord with the macro management direction and contribute to a more balanced external economy. With the continuous perfection of the RMB exchange rate formation mechanism and less intervention in the foreign exchange market by the central bank, the current BOP pattern of a current account surplus and a capital and financial account deficit will continue and boost private-sector foreign exchange investment. Meanwhile, in the context of the slow recovery of the global economy and the increased turbulence in international financial markets, China, an increasingly more open economy, cannot possibly be immune from cross-border capital flow fluctuations. Specifically, when China's BOP and RMB exchange rate tend to reach an equilibrium, two-way cross-border capital flows become unavoidable. However, due to its relatively rapid GDP growth, its persistent surplus of trade in goods, its large foreign exchange reserve assets, and its more stable FDI inflows rather than volatile portfolio inflows, China is able to sustain the cross-border capital flow shocks.

In the second half of 2012, China's BOP is projected to remain in balance. Meanwhile, several unsteady and uncertain external factors will continue to exist. For example, although the US economy may improve, the "fiscal cliff" may possibly trigger a fiscal tightening. Also, the Euro area as a whole is at an early stage of deleveraging, and the Euro sovereign debt crisis might deepen. Moreover, due to changes in the external economic environment, the emerging market economies are facing both supply and demand pressures. In addition, we should not ignore the possible occurrence of geo-political events. But some positive factors are gradually accumulating, possibly contributing to a more balanced BOP in China. First, the nation has put more focus on steady growth. The most recent pre-set and fine-tuning adjustment policies are aimed to stimulate market confidence and maintain steady GDP growth. Second, China will maintain a relatively large surplus for trade in goods in the second half of 2012. Due to the sluggish world economy, the decrease in international prices of bulk commodity will also reduce China's costs of imports. Third, as the major economies pay more attention to economic growth, these countries and areas will still have the resources and determination to prevent an exacerbation of the debt crisis. In sum, if there are no unexpected domestic and international events, China will achieve a relatively balanced BOP in 2012.

Box 6

The Status Quo and the Impact of the Euro Sovereign Debt Crisis

The European sovereign debt crisis began in Greece in 2009. After that Greece announced its inability to repay its sovereign debt, the long-existing structural conflicts in Europe erupted, characterized by an aging demography, high social security benefits, an inflexible labor market, and a unified currency but independent fiscal policies of the member countries. With the high cost but low efficiency in economic policy coordination and the eruption of the European sovereign debt crisis, the mixture of a sovereign debt crisis, banking crisis, economic and political crisis, and social crisis developed into an omni-directional systemic crisis.

Since the beginning of 2012, the European crisis has gone through improving, deteriorating, and mitigating stages. In the first quarter, the European Central Bank (ECB) allotted 529.5 billion Euro in the second round of the three-year LTRO. The European Union Summit signed a fiscal treaty, namely the Treaty on Stability, Coordination and Governance in the Economic and Monetary Union. The above measures helped to reinforce the EU's fiscal discipline and surveillance, to ease the liquidity shortage in the European banking system, and to boost market confidence. However, in the second quarter, when Spain's fiscal deficit deteriorated and new problems such as the capital inadequacy of the European banks emerged, sovereign bond prices in Spain and Italy dropped sharply. Several European banks with a large European sovereign debt position were also downgraded. All these factors led to another deterioration in the European debt crisis. To combat the crisis, EU launched a set of rescue measures, including offering a 100-billion-Euro aid loan to Spain, promoting a banking union, and launching a 120-billion-Euro stimulus growth plan. However, these measures only mitigated the progression of the crisis and did not resolve the key problems. In July, the Greece Rescue Negotiation was at a standstill, and Spain's local government debt problem was revealed. In September, the Netherlands will hold a general election. Because of the public's general dissatisfaction with the EU's tightening plans, the Netherlands may vote for a government that will possibly deviate from the EU's budgetary constraints at the expense of the country's AAA rating. Also in September, the German Court will decide upon the legality of the European

Stability Mechanism. If the decision is not accepted by the public, Germany will possibly hold a referendum. These factors cast a shadow on the future of the European sovereign debt crisis.

In light of the fact that the EU is the largest economy and the Euro zone is the largest unitary currency area in the world, and that the Euro is the second largest international reserve currency after the US dollar, the European sovereign debt crisis has a great impact on European and global economic and financial developments. After the breakout of the crisis, the GDP growth rate in the EU was projected to drop from 2.0 percent in 2010 to 0 percent in 2012. The rate of unemployment rose from 9.7 percent in 2010 to 10.4 percent in June 2012. The EU government debt to GDP rose from 80.0 percent in 2010 to the current 83.4 percent. As the recession and the downgrading in the sovereign ratings persist, the EU countries have become involved in a vicious circle of fiscal tightening, economic recession, and heavier debt burdens, and then another round of fiscal tightening. At the international level, the foreign trade of the EU decreased, which greatly affected the EU's trade counterparties. As to financial markets, the stability of the Euro zone was under attack. The Euro-USD exchange rate depreciated from 1.3583 at the end of 2010 to the current 1.2814. Both the stock and bond markets experienced drastic turbulence. As a result, several European financial institutions with large European debt positions experienced a great loss of assets. The loan business of banks stagnated. The economic and financial crisis also adversely affected European political and social conditions, causing continuous internal conflicts among the EU countries and disputes regarding the EU integration progress. The long economic recession and high unemployment also led to great public dissatisfaction, contributing to frequent government changes and more social turbulence.

In the second half of 2012, the foreign exchange administration authority will follow the unified arrangements of the Party Central Committee and the State Council, stick to the improving-through-steady-progress macro-management plan and focus more on steady growth. It will also firmly stick to a risk baseline and further improve its capacity to serve the real economy and to maintain the nation's economic and financial safety. The major tasks are to: first, firmly stick to a risk baseline, closely monitor trends in cross-border cash flows and improve policy plans, and avoid and resolve potential risks in the field of foreign exchange management; second, further facilitate trade and investment, promote nationwide foreign exchange administrative reforms on trade in goods, steadily promote development of the system of Qualified Domestic Institutional Investors (QDIIs) and Qualified Foreign Institutional Investors (QFIIs); third, accelerate foreign exchange market development, enrich RMB foreign exchange derivatives products, improve the market-maker mechanism, and strengthen the self-adjusting and balancing ability of the foreign exchange market; and fourth, strengthen and improve foreign exchange reserve management in order to maintain the safety of national reserve assets.

附　录 统计资料
Appendix　Statistics

一、国际收支①

I. Balance of Payments

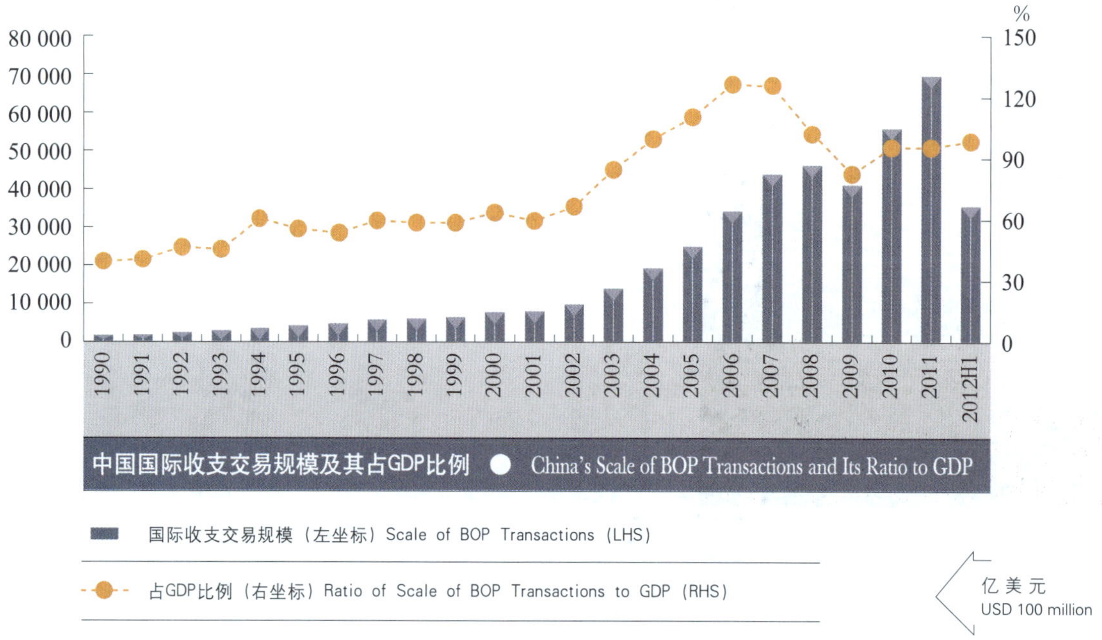

中国国际收支交易规模及其占GDP比例 ● China's Scale of BOP Transactions and Its Ratio to GDP

①资料来源：国家外汇管理局；路透；《国际收支统计》、《国际金融统计》；CEIC Asia Database。
Sources: State Administration of Foreign Exchange; Reuters, Balance of Payments Statistics, International Financial Statistics; CEIC Asia Database.

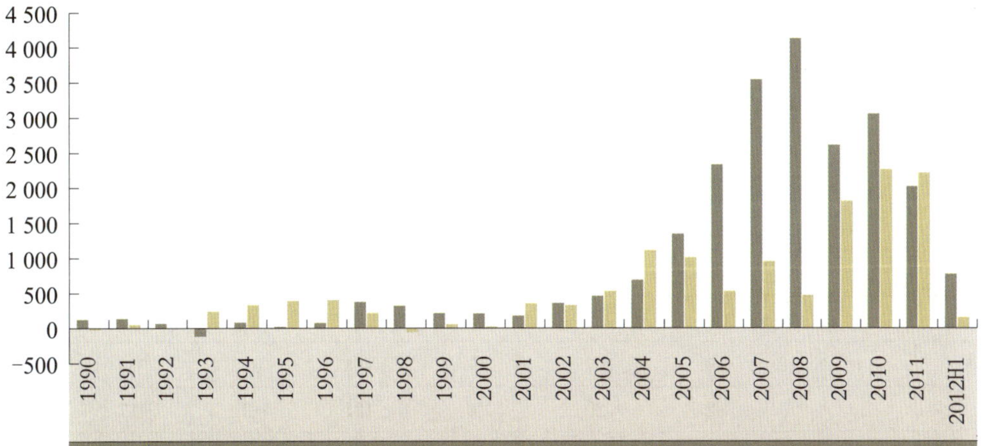

中国经常项目差额与资本和金融项目差额
China's Current Account Balance & Capital and Financial Account Balance

■ 经常项目差额 Current Account Balance

■ 资本和金融项目差额 Capital and Financial Account Balance

亿美元
USD 100 million

中国国际收支概览表（1）

China's Balance of Payments Abridged

项目 Item / 年份 Year	1982	1983	1984	1985	1986	1987	1988
一、经常账户差额 Current Account Balance	**57**	**42**	**20**	**−114**	**−70**	**3**	**−38**
贷方 Credit	254	254	293	301	312	405	479
借方 Debit	197	211	273	415	382	402	518
A.货物和服务差额 Goods and Services Balance	**48**	**26**	**1**	**−125**	**−74**	**3**	**−41**
贷方 Credit	237	233	268	283	298	392	459
借方 Debit	189	207	267	408	372	389	500
a.货物差额 Goods Balance	**42**	**20**	**0**	**−131**	**−91**	**−17**	**−53**
贷方 Credit	211	207	239	251	258	347	411
借方 Debit	169	187	239	382	349	364	464
b.服务差额 Services Balance	**6**	**6**	**0**	**6**	**18**	**20**	**13**
贷方 Credit	**26**	**26**	**29**	**31**	**40**	**44**	**49**
借方 Debit	**20**	**20**	**29**	**25**	**23**	**25**	**36**
B.收益差额 Income Balance	**4**	**12**	**15**	**8**	**−0**	**−2**	**−2**
贷方 Credit	10	15	19	14	9	10	15
借方 Debit	6	3	4	5	9	12	16
C.经常转移差额 Current Transfers Balance	**5**	**5**	**4**	**2**	**4**	**2**	**4**
贷方 Credit	7	6	6	4	5	4	6
借方 Debit	2	1	2	2	1	2	1
二、资本和金融项目差额 Capital and Financial Account Balance	**−17**	**−14**	**−38**	**85**	**65**	**27**	**53**
贷方 Credit	36	30	45	212	213	192	203
借方 Debit	53	44	83	127	148	164	150
A.资本账户差额 Capital Account Balance	—	—	—	—	—	—	—
贷方 Credit	—	—	—	—	—	—	—
借方 Debit	—	—	—	—	—	—	—
B.金融账户差额 Financial Account Balance	**−17**	**−14**	**−38**	**85**	**65**	**27**	**53**
贷方 Credit	36	30	45	212	213	192	203
借方 Debit	53	44	83	127	148	164	150

单位：亿美元
Unit: USD 100 million

项目 Item | 年份 Year	1982	1983	1984	1985	1986	1987	1988
1.直接投资差额 Direct Investment Balance	**4**	**8**	**13**	**13**	**18**	**17**	**23**
贷方 Credit	4	9	14	20	22	23	32
借方 Debit	0	1	1	6	5	6	9
2.证券投资差额 Portfolio Investment Balance	**0**	**−6**	**−16**	**30**	**16**	**11**	**9**
贷方 Credit	0	2	9	30	16	12	12
借方 Debit	0	8	26	0	0	1	3
3.其他投资差额 Other Investment Balance	**−21**	**−16**	**−34**	**41**	**32**	**0**	**20**
贷方 Credit	31	20	22	162	175	157	159
借方 Debit	52	35	56	120	143	157	138
三、储备资产变动额 Reserve Assets	**−42**	**−27**	**5**	**54**	**17**	**−17**	**−5**
贷方 Credit	1	—	7	56	19	—	1
借方 Debit	43	27	2	2	1	17	5
其中：外汇储备差额 Foreign Exchange Reserves	−43	−19	7	56	12	−15	−4
四、净误差与遗漏 Net Errors and Omissions	**3**	**−2**	**12**	**−25**	**−12**	**−14**	**−10**

中国国际收支概览表（2）

China's Balance of Payments Abridged

项目 Item | 年份 Year	1989	1990	1991	1992	1993	1994
一、经常账户差额 Current Account Balance	**−43**	**120**	**133**	**64**	**−119**	**77**
贷方 Credit	502	608	705	856	922	1 264
借方 Debit	545	488	572	792	1 041	1 188
A.货物和服务差额 Goods and Services Balance	**−49**	**107**	**116**	**50**	**−118**	**74**
贷方 Credit	478	574	659	788	866	1 189
借方 Debit	528	467	543	738	983	1 116
a.货物差额 Goods Balance	**−56**	**92**	**87**	**52**	**−107**	**73**
贷方 Credit	432	515	589	696	757	1 026
借方 Debit	488	424	502	644	863	953
b.服务差额 Services Balance	**7**	**15**	**29**	**−2**	**−11**	**1**
贷方 Credit	46	59	70	92	109	164
借方 Debit	39	44	41	94	120	163
B.收益差额 Income Balance	**2**	**11**	**8**	**2**	**−13**	**−10**
贷方 Credit	19	30	37	56	44	57
借方 Debit	17	20	29	53	57	68
C.经常转移差额 Current Transfers Balance	**4**	**3**	**8**	**12**	**12**	**13**
贷方 Credit	5	4	9	12	13	18
借方 Debit	1	1	1	1	1	4
二、资本和金融项目差额 Capital and Financial Account Balance	**64**	**−28**	**46**	**−3**	**235**	**326**
贷方 Credit	212	204	203	302	508	618
借方 Debit	148	232	157	305	274	291
A.资本账户差额 Capital Account Balance	—	—	—	—	—	—
贷方 Credit	—	—	—	—	—	—
借方 Debit	—	—	—	—	—	—
B.金融账户差额 Financial Account Balance	**64**	**−28**	**46**	**−3**	**235**	**326**
贷方 Credit	212	204	203	302	508	618
借方 Debit	148	232	157	305	274	291

单位：亿美元
Unit: USD 100 million

项目 Item / 年份 Year	1989	1990	1991	1992	1993	1994
1.直接投资差额 Direct Investment Balance	**26**	**27**	**35**	**72**	**231**	**318**
贷方 Credit	34	35	44	112	275	338
借方 Debit	8	8	9	40	44	20
2.证券投资差额 Portfolio Investment Balance	**−2**	**−2**	**2**	**−1**	**31**	**35**
贷方 Credit	1	—	6	9	50	45
借方 Debit	3	2	3	9	20	10
3.其他投资差额 Other Investment Balance	**40**	**−52**	**9**	**−74**	**−27**	**−27**
贷方 Credit	177	169	154	182	183	235
借方 Debit	137	221	145	256	210	262
三、储备资产变动额 Reserve Assets	**−22**	**−61**	**−111**	**21**	**−18**	**−305**
贷方 Credit	1	—	—	24	1	—
借方 Debit	23	61	111	3	18	305
其中：外汇储备差额 Foreign Exchange Reserves	−22	−55	−106	23	−18	−304
四、净误差与遗漏 Net Errors and Omissions	**1**	**−31**	**−68**	**−83**	**−98**	**−98**

中国国际收支概览表（3）

China's Balance of Payments Abridged

项目 Item / 年份 Year	1995	1996	1997	1998	1999	2000
一、经常账户差额 Current Account Balance	**16**	**72**	**370**	**315**	**211**	**205**
贷方 Credit	1 543	1 814	2 184	2 177	2 347	2 990
借方 Debit	1 526	1 741	1 815	1 862	2 135	2 785
A.货物和服务差额 Goods and Services Balance	**120**	**176**	**428**	**438**	**306**	**289**
贷方 Credit	1 472	1 717	2 072	2 074	2 210	2 796
借方 Debit	1 353	1 541	1 644	1 636	1 903	2 507
a.货物差额 Goods Balance	**181**	**195**	**462**	**466**	**360**	**345**
贷方 Credit	1 281	1 511	1 827	1 835	1 947	2 491
借方 Debit	1 101	1 315	1 364	1 369	1 587	2 147
b.服务差额 Services Balance	**−61**	**−20**	**−34**	**−28**	**−53**	**−56**
贷方 Credit	191	206	246	239	262	304
借方 Debit	252	226	280	267	316	360
B.收益差额 Income Balance	**−118**	**−124**	**−110**	**−166**	**−145**	**−147**
贷方 Credit	52	73	57	56	83	126
借方 Debit	170	198	167	222	228	272
C.经常转移差额 Current Transfers Balance	**14**	**21**	**51**	**43**	**49**	**63**
贷方 Credit	18	24	55	47	54	69
借方 Debit	4	2	3	4	4	5
二、资本和金融项目差额 Capital and Financial Account Balance	**387**	**400**	**210**	**−63**	**52**	**19**
贷方 Credit	677	710	926	893	918	920
借方 Debit	290	310	716	956	866	901
A.资本账户差额 Capital Account Balance	—	—	**0**	**0**	**0**	**0**
贷方 Credit	—	—	—	—	—	—
借方 Debit	—	—	0	0	0	0
B.金融账户差额 Financial Account Balance	**387**	**400**	**210**	**−63**	**52**	**20**
贷方 Credit	677	710	926	893	918	920
借方 Debit	290	310	716	956	865	900

单位：亿美元
Unit: USD 100 million

项目 Item / 年份 Year	1995	1996	1997	1998	1999	2000
1.直接投资差额 Direct Investment Balance	**338**	**381**	**417**	**411**	**370**	**375**
贷方 Credit	377	424	454	456	410	421
借方 Debit	39	43	38	45	40	46
2.证券投资差额 Portfolio Investment Balance	**8**	**17**	**69**	**-37**	**-112**	**-40**
贷方 Credit	18	34	92	19	18	78
借方 Debit	10	16	23	56	130	118
3.其他投资差额 Other Investment Balance	**40**	**2**	**-276**	**-437**	**-205**	**-315**
贷方 Credit	282	253	380	418	489	421
借方 Debit	241	251	655	854	695	736
三、储备资产变动额 Reserve Assets	**-225**	**-317**	**-357**	**-64**	**-85**	**-105**
贷方 Credit	—	—	0	—	13	4
借方 Debit	225	317	357	64	98	110
其中：外汇储备差额 Foreign Exchange Reserves	-220	-315	-349	-51	-97	-109
四、净误差与遗漏 Net Errors and Omissions	**-178**	**-155**	**-223**	**-187**	**-178**	**-119**

中国国际收支概览表（4）

China's Balance of Payments Abridged

项目 Item | 年份 Year	2001	2002	2003	2004	2005	2006
一、经常账户差额 Current Account Balance	**174**	**354**	**459**	**687**	**1 341**	**2 327**
贷方 Credit	3 179	3 875	5 196	7 007	9 036	11 479
借方 Debit	3 005	3 521	4 737	6 320	7 695	9 152
A.货物和服务差额 Goods and Services Balance	**281**	**374**	**361**	**493**	**1 248**	**2 089**
贷方 Credit	2 994	3 654	4 850	6 558	8 369	10 617
借方 Debit	2 713	3 280	4 489	6 065	7 121	8 528
a.货物差额 Goods Balance	**340**	**442**	**447**	**590**	**1 342**	**2 177**
贷方 Credit	2 661	3 257	4 383	5 934	7 625	9 697
借方 Debit	2 321	2 815	3 936	5 344	6 283	7 519
b.服务差额 Services Balance	**−59**	**−68**	**−86**	**−97**	**−94**	**−88**
贷方 Credit	333	397	467	624	744	920
借方 Debit	393	465	553	721	838	1 008
B.收益差额 Income Balance	**−192**	**−149**	**−78**	**−35**	**−161**	**−54**
贷方 Credit	94	83	161	205	390	546
借方 Debit	286	233	239	241	551	600
C.经常转移差额 Current Transfers Balance	**85**	**130**	**176**	**229**	**254**	**292**
贷方 Credit	91	138	185	243	277	316
借方 Debit	6	8	8	14	23	24
二、资本和金融项目差额 Capital and Financial Account Balance	**348**	**323**	**527**	**1 107**	**1 010**	**526**
贷方 Credit	995	1 283	2 196	3 434	4 570	6 993
借方 Debit	648	960	1 669	2 327	3 560	6 466
A.资本账户差额 Capital Account Balance	**−1**	**0**	**0**	**−1**	**41**	**40**
贷方 Credit	—	—	—	—	42	41
借方 Debit	1	0	0	1	1	1
B.金融账户差额 Financial Account Balance	**348**	**323**	**528**	**1 107**	**969**	**486**
贷方 Credit	995	1 283	2 196	3 434	4 529	6 952
借方 Debit	647	960	1 669	2 326	3 559	6 465

单位：亿美元
Unit: USD 100 million

项目 Item / 年份 Year	2001	2002	2003	2004	2005	2006
1.直接投资差额 Direct Investment Balance	**374**	**468**	**472**	**531**	**1 059**	**1 029**
贷方 Credit	471	531	555	609	1 242	1 333
借方 Debit	97	63	83	78	183	304
2.证券投资差额 Portfolio Investment Balance	**−194**	**−103**	**114**	**197**	**−49**	**−676**
贷方 Credit	24	23	123	203	220	456
借方 Debit	218	126	9	6	269	1 132
3.其他投资差额 Other Investment Balance	**169**	**−41**	**−59**	**379**	**−40**	**133**
贷方 Credit	501	730	1 518	2 622	3 067	5 163
借方 Debit	332	771	1 577	2 243	3 108	5 030
三、储备资产变动额 Reserve Assets	**−473**	**−755**	**−1 379**	**−1 901**	**−2 506**	**−2 848**
贷方 Credit	—	—	—	5	19	5
借方 Debit	473	755	1 379	1 905	2 526	2 853
其中：外汇储备差额 Foreign Exchange Reserves	−466	−742	−1 377	−1 904	−2 526	−2 853
四、净误差与遗漏 Net Errors and Omissions	**−49**	**78**	**393**	**107**	**155**	**−6**

中国国际收支概览表（5）

China's Balance of Payments Abridged

项目 Item / 年份 Year	2007	2008	2009	2010	2011	2012H1
一、经常账户差额 Current Account Balance	**3 540**	**4 124**	**2 611**	**2 378**	**2 017**	**772**
贷方 Credit	14 679	17 359	14 846	19 355	22 868	11 636
借方 Debit	11 139	13 235	12 235	16 977	20 851	10 863
A.货物和服务差额 Goods and Services Balance	**3 075**	**3 489**	**2 201**	**2 230**	**1 883**	**726**
贷方 Credit	13 422	15 817	13 333	17 436	20 867	10 480
借方 Debit	10 347	12 328	11 132	15 206	18 983	9 754
a.货物差额 Goods Balance	**3 154**	**3 607**	**2 495**	**2 542**	**2 435**	**1 128**
贷方 Credit	12 200	14 346	12 038	15 814	19 038	9 577
借方 Debit	9 046	10 739	9 543	13 272	16 603	8 449
b.服务差额 Services Balance	**−79**	**−118**	**−294**	**−312**	**−552**	**−403**
贷方 Credit	1 222	1 471	1 295	1 622	1 828	903
借方 Debit	1 301	1 589	1 589	1 933	2 381	1 305
B.收益差额 Income Balance	**79**	**177**	**73**	**−259**	**−119**	**16**
贷方 Credit	830	1 016	1 086	1 424	1 446	902
借方 Debit	752	839	1 013	1 683	1 565	885
C.经常转移差额 Current Transfers Balance	**387**	**458**	**337**	**407**	**253**	**31**
贷方 Credit	426	526	426	495	556	255
借方 Debit	40	68	89	88	303	224
二、资本和金融项目差额 Capital and Financial Account Balance	**951**	**463**	**1 808**	**2 869**	**2 211**	**149**
贷方 Credit	9 436	7 972	7 825	11 667	13 982	6 527
借方 Debit	8 485	7 509	6 016	8 798	11 772	6 378
A.资本账户差额 Capital Account Balance	**31**	**31**	**40**	**46**	**54**	**24**
贷方 Credit	33	33	42	48	56	25
借方 Debit	2	3	2	2	2	1
B.金融账户差额 Financial Account Balance	**920**	**433**	**1 769**	**2 822**	**2 156**	**125**
贷方 Credit	9 403	7 939	7 783	11 618	13 926	6 501
借方 Debit	8 482	7 506	6 014	8 796	11 770	6 377

单位：亿美元
Unit: USD 100 million

项目 Item | 年份 Year	2007	2008	2009	2010	2011	2012H1
1.直接投资差额 Direct Investment Balance	**1 431**	**1 217**	**703**	**1 857**	**1 704**	**900**
贷方 Credit	1 732	1 904	1 502	2 730	2 717	1 414
借方 Debit	301	687	799	872	1 012	514
2.证券投资差额 Portfolio Investment Balance	**187**	**427**	**387**	**240**	**196**	**204**
贷方 Credit	640	677	981	636	519	310
借方 Debit	453	250	594	395	323	106
3.其他投资差额 Other Investment Balance	**−697**	**−1 211**	**679**	**724**	**255**	**−979**
贷方 Credit	7 031	5 358	5 299	8 253	10 690	4 778
借方 Debit	7 728	6 569	4 620	7 528	10 435	5 757
三、储备资产变动额 Reserve Assets	**−4 607**	**−4 795**	**−3 984**	**−4 717**	**−3 878**	**−629**
贷方 Credit	2	—	—	—	10	121
借方 Debit	4 609	4 795	3 984	4 717	3 888	750
其中：外汇储备差额 Foreign Exchange Reserves	−4 609	−4 783	−3 821	−4 696	−3 848	−636
四、净误差与遗漏 Net Errors and Omissions	**116**	**209**	**−435**	**−529**	**−350**	**−292**

2012年上半年中国国际收支平衡表

China's Balance of Payments in the First Half of 2012

项目 Item	差 额 Balance	贷 方 Credit	借 方 Debit
一、经常项目Current Account	**772**	**11 636**	**10 863**
A.货物和服务Goods and Services	**726**	**10 480**	**9 754**
a.货物Goods	**1 128**	**9 577**	**8 449**
b.服务Services	**−403**	**903**	**1 305**
1.运输Transportation	−229	184	414
2.旅游Travel	−218	238	456
3.通讯服务Communication Services	3	9	6
4.建筑服务Construction Services	46	61	15
5.保险服务Insurance Services	−84	17	100
6.金融服务Financial Services	−1	4	5
7.计算机和信息服务Computer and Information Services	53	69	16
8.专有权利使用费和特许费Royalties and Licensing Fees	−85	4	89
9.咨询Consulting Service	66	157	91
10.广告、宣传Advertising and Public Opinion Polling	9	23	14
11.电影、音像Audio-visual and Related Services	−2	1	2
12.其他商业服务Other Business Services	40	132	92
13.别处未提及的政府服务Government Services, n.i.e	−1	4	5
B.收益Income	**16**	**902**	**885**
1.职工报酬Compensation of Employee	73	82	9
2.投资收益Investment Income	−57	820	876
C.经常转移Current Transfers	**31**	**255**	**224**
1.各级政府General Government	−15	4	19
2.其他部门Other Sectors	46	250	205
二、资本和金融项目Capital and Financial Account	**149**	**6 527**	**6 378**
A.资本项目Capital Account	**24**	**25**	**1**
B.金融项目Financial Account	**125**	**6 501**	**6 377**
1.直接投资Direct Investment	**900**	**1 414**	**514**
1.1 我国在外直接投资Direct Investment Abroad	−281	100	380
1.2 外国在华直接投资Direct Investment in China	1 181	1 314	133
2.证券投资Portfolio Investment	**204**	**310**	**106**
2.1 资产Assets	59	143	85
2.1.1 股本证券Equity Securities	22	50	28
2.1.2 债务证券Debt Securities	36	93	57
2.1.2.1 (中)长期债券Bonds and Notes	52	87	35
2.1.2.2 货币市场工具Money Market Instruments	−16	6	22
2.2 负债Liabilities	145	166	21
2.2.1 股本证券Equity Securities	53	74	21
2.2.2 债务证券Debt Securities	92	92	0
2.2.2.1 (中)长期债券Bonds and Notes	71	71	0
2.2.2.2 货币市场工具Money Market Instruments	21	21	0
3.其他投资Other Investment	**−979**	**4 778**	**5 757**
3.1 资产Assets	−1 623	265	1 887
3.1.1 贸易信贷Trade Credits	−332	4	336

单位：亿美元
Unit: USD 100 million

项目 Item	差 额 Balance	贷 方 Credit	借 方 Debit
长期Long-term	−7	0	7
短期Short-term	−326	4	330
3.1.2 贷款Loans	−431	7	438
长期Long-term	−183	0	183
短期Short-term	−248	7	255
3.1.3 货币和存款Currency and Deposits	−967	146	1 113
3.1.4 其他资产Other Assets	108	108	0
长期Long-term	0	0	0
短期Short-term	108	108	0
3.2 负债Liabilities	644	4 513	3 870
3.2.1 贸易信贷Trade Credits	409	409	0
长期Long-term	7	7	0
短期Short-term	402	402	0
3.2.2 贷款Loans	379	3 394	3 015
长期Long-term	87	245	158
短期Short-term	292	3 149	2 857
3.2.3 货币和存款Currency and Deposits	−183	658	841
3.2.4 其他负债Other Liabilities	39	53	14
长期Long-term	43	43	0
短期Short-term	−4	10	14
三、储备资产Reserve Assets	**−629**	**121**	**750**
1. 货币黄金Monetary Gold	0	0	0
2. 特别提款权Special Drawing Rights	−1	1	2
3. 在基金组织的储备头寸Reserve Position in the Fund	8	8	0
4. 外汇Foreign Exchange	−636	0	636
5. 其他债权Other Claims	0	0	0
四、净误差与遗漏Net Errors and Omissions	**−292**	**0**	**292**

中国国际投资头寸表

China's International Investment Position

项目 Item	2006年末 End-2006	2007年末 End-2007	2008年末 End-2008	2009年末 End-2009	2010年末 End-2010	2011年末 End-2011	2012年6月末 End-Jun. 2012
净头寸Net	**6 402**	**11 881**	**14 938**	**14 905**	**16 880**	**17 747**	**17 488**
A.资产Assets	**16 905**	**24 162**	**29 567**	**34 369**	**41 189**	**47 182**	**49 462**
1.在国外直接投资Direct Investment Abroad	**906**	**1 160**	**1 857**	**2 458**	**3 172**	**3 642**	**3 923**
2.证券投资Portfolio Investment	**2 652**	**2 846**	**2 525**	**2 428**	**2 571**	**2 600**	**2 593**
2.1股本证券Equity Securities	15	196	214	546	630	619	1 006
2.2债务证券Debt Securities	2 637	2 650	2 311	1 882	1 941	1 981	1 587
3.其他投资Other Investment	**2 539**	**4 683**	**5 523**	**4 952**	**6 304**	**8 382**	**9 798**
3.1贸易信贷Trade Credits	922	1 160	1 102	1 444	2 060	2 769	3 101
3.2贷款Loans	670	888	1 071	974	1 174	2 232	2 671
3.3货币和存款Currency and Deposits	736	1 380	1 529	1 310	2 051	2 829	3 577
3.4其他资产Other Assets	210	1 255	1 821	1 224	1 018	552	448
4.储备资产Reserve assets	**10 808**	**15 473**	**19 662**	**24 532**	**29 142**	**32 558**	**33 148**
4.1货币黄金Monetary Gold	123	170	169	371	481	530	542
4.2特别提款权Special Drawing Rights	11	12	12	125	123	119	118
4.3在基金组织中的储备头寸Reserve Position in the Fund	11	8	20	44	64	98	88
4.4外汇Foreign Exchange	10 663	15 282	19 460	23 992	28 473	31 811	32 400

单位：亿美元
Unit: USD 100 million

项目 Item	2006年末 End-2006	2007年末 End-2007	2008年末 End-2008	2009年末 End-2009	2010年末 End-2010	2011年末 End-2011	2012年6月末 End-Jun. 2012
B.负债Liabilities	**10 503**	**12 281**	**14 629**	**19 464**	**24 308**	**29 434**	**31 974**
1.外国来华直接投资Direct Investment in Reporting Economy	**6 144**	**7 037**	**9 155**	**13 148**	**15 696**	**18 042**	**19 032**
2.证券投资Portfolio Investment	**1 207**	**1 466**	**1 677**	**1 900**	**2 239**	**2 485**	**3 011**
2.1股本证券Equity Securities	1 065	1 290	1 505	1 748	2 061	2 114	2 469
2.2债务证券Debt Securities	142	176	172	152	178	371	542
3.其他投资Other Investment	**3 152**	**3 778**	**3 796**	**4 416**	**6 373**	**8 907**	**9 932**
3.1贸易信贷Trade Credits	1 196	1 487	1 296	1 617	2 112	2 492	2 901
3.2贷款Loans	985	1 033	1 030	1 636	2 389	3 724	4 110
3.3货币和存款Currency and Deposits	595	791	918	937	1 650	2 477	2 580
3.4其他负债Other Liabilities	377	467	552	227	222	214	341

外汇储备

Foreign Exchange Reserves

单位：亿美元
Unit: USD 100 million

年份 Year	外汇储备余额 Foreign Exchange Reserves	外汇储备增加额 Increase of Foreign Exchange Reserves
1990	111	55
1991	217	106
1992	194	−23
1993	212	18
1994	516	304
1995	736	220
1996	1 050	315
1997	1 399	348
1998	1 450	51
1999	1 547	97
2000	1 656	109
2001	2 122	466
2002	2 864	742
2003	4 033	1 168
2004	6 099	2 067
2005	8 189	2 090
2006	10 663	2 475
2007	15 282	4 619
2008	19 460	4 178
2009	23 992	4 531
2010	28 473	4 481
2011	31 811	3 338
2012H1	32 400	589

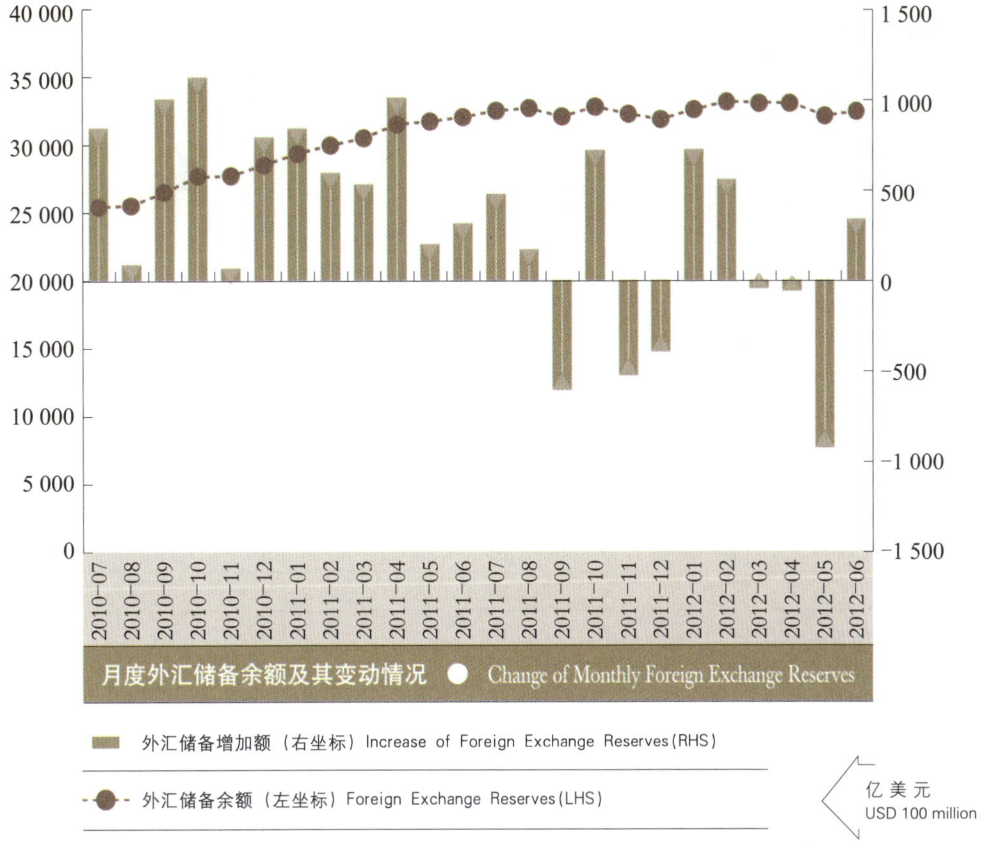

月度外汇储备余额及其变动情况 ● Change of Monthly Foreign Exchange Reserves

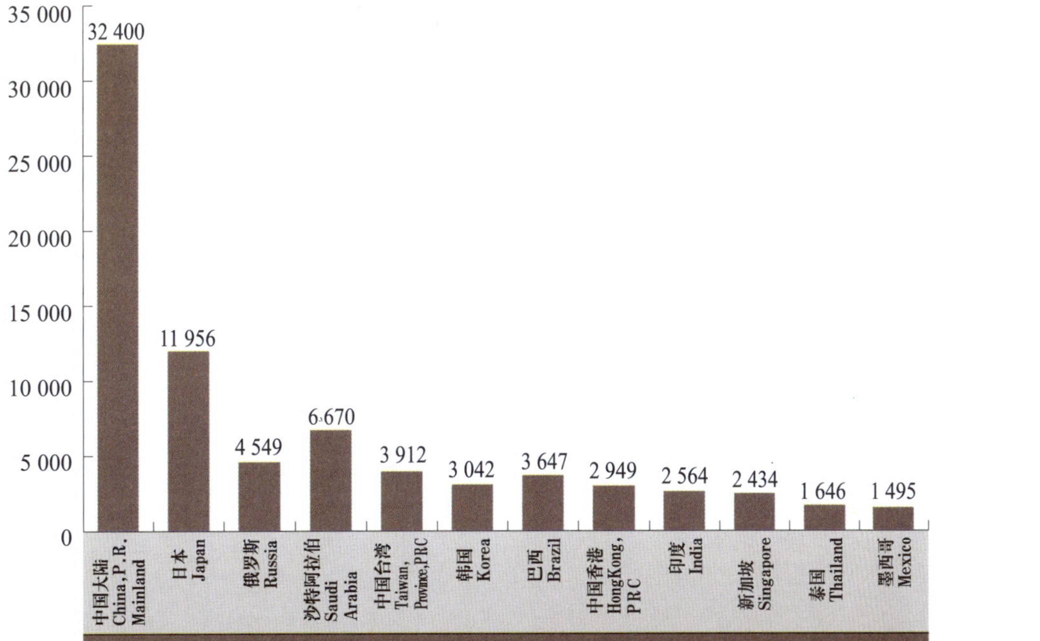

2012年6月末部分国家和地区外汇储备 ● Foreign Reserves of Some Countries/ Regions, End of Jun.2012

二、对外贸易[①]

Ⅱ. Foreign Trade

2011年世界货物贸易出口前十名

Top 10 Countries/Regions of Goods Export in 2011

国家/地区 Countries/Regions	出口额（10亿美元） Export（USD billion）	增长 Increase（%）	占世界出口总额比重 Ratio to Total Export of the World（%）	2010年排名 Ranking in 2010
世界World	18 215	15	100.0	
1.中国PRC	1 899	20	10.4	1
2.美国U.S.A	1 481	16	8.1	2
3.德国Germany	1 474	17	8.1	3
4.日本Japan	823	7	4.5	4
5.荷兰Netherlands	660	15	3.6	5
6.法国France	597	14	3.3	6
7.韩国Korea	555	19	3.0	7
8.意大利Italy	523	17	2.9	8
9.俄罗斯Russian	522	30	2.9	12
10.比利时Belgium	476	17	2.6	9

①资料来源：海关总署；世界贸易组织。
Sources: General Administration of Customs; World Trade Organization.

2011年世界货物贸易进口前十名

Top 10 Countries/Regions of Goods Import in 2011

国家/地区 Countries/Regions	进口额（10亿美元） Import（USD billion）	增长 Increase（%）	占世界进口总额比重 Ratio to Total Import of the World（%）	2010年排名 Ranking in 2010
世界World	18 380	19	100.0	
1.美国U.S.A	2 265	15	12.3	1
2.中国PRC	1 743	25	9.5	2
3.德国Germany	1 254	19	6.8	3
4.日本Japan	854	23	4.6	5
5.法国France	714	17	3.9	4
6.英国UK	636	13	3.5	6
7.荷兰Netherlands	597	16	3.2	7
8.意大利Italy	557	14	3.0	8
9.韩国Korea	525	23	2.9	10
10.中国香港HongKong，PRC	511	16	2.8	9

中国进出口总值

China's Total Value of Import & Export

单位：亿美元
Unit: USD 100 million

年度 Year	进出口 Import & Export	出口 Export	进口 Import	差额 Balance
1981	440	220	220	0
1982	416	223	193	30
1983	436	222	214	8
1984	535	261	274	−13
1985	696	274	423	−149
1986	738	309	429	−120
1987	827	394	432	−38
1988	1 028	475	553	−78
1989	1 117	525	591	−66
1990	1 154	621	534	87
1991	1 357	719	638	81
1992	1 655	849	806	44
1993	1 957	917	1 040	−122
1994	2 366	1 210	1 156	54
1995	2 809	1 488	1 321	167
1996	2 899	1 511	1 388	122
1997	3 252	1 828	1 424	404
1998	3 239	1 837	1 402	435
1999	3 606	1 949	1 657	292
2000	4 743	2 492	2 251	241
2001	5 097	2 661	2 436	226
2002	6 208	3 256	2 952	304
2003	8 510	4 382	4 128	255
2004	11 546	5 933	5 612	321
2005	14 219	7 620	6 600	1 020
2006	17 604	9 689	7 915	1 775
2007	21 766	12 205	9 561	2 643
2008	25 633	14 307	11 326	2 981
2009	22 072	12 017	10 059	1 957
2010	29 728	15 779	13 948	1 831
2011	36 421	18 986	17 435	1 551
2012H1	18 398	9 544	8 855	689

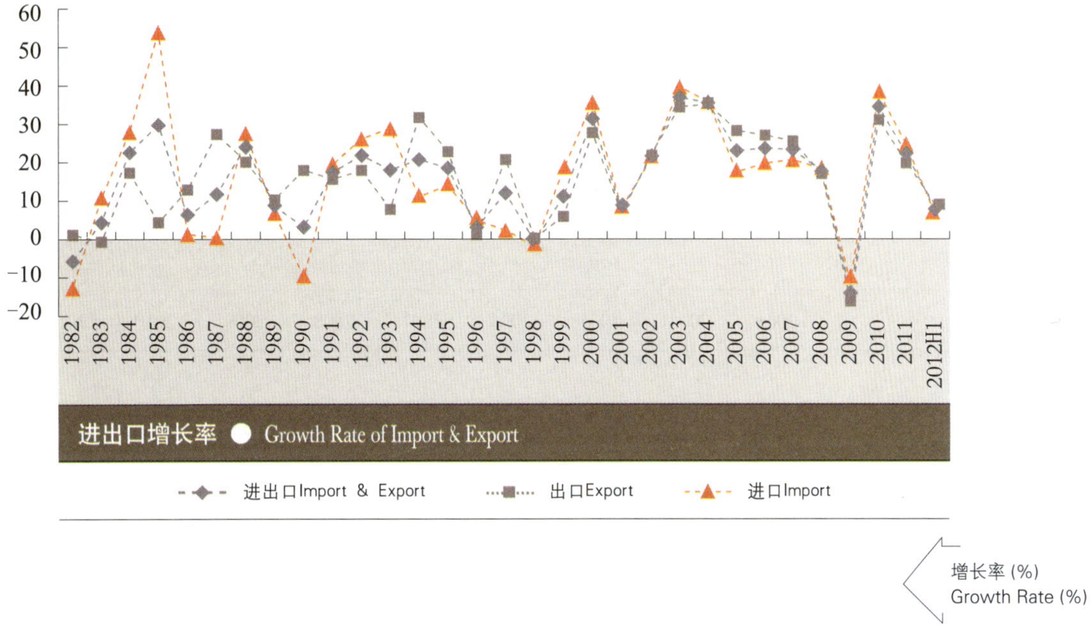

进出口增长率 ● Growth Rate of Import & Export

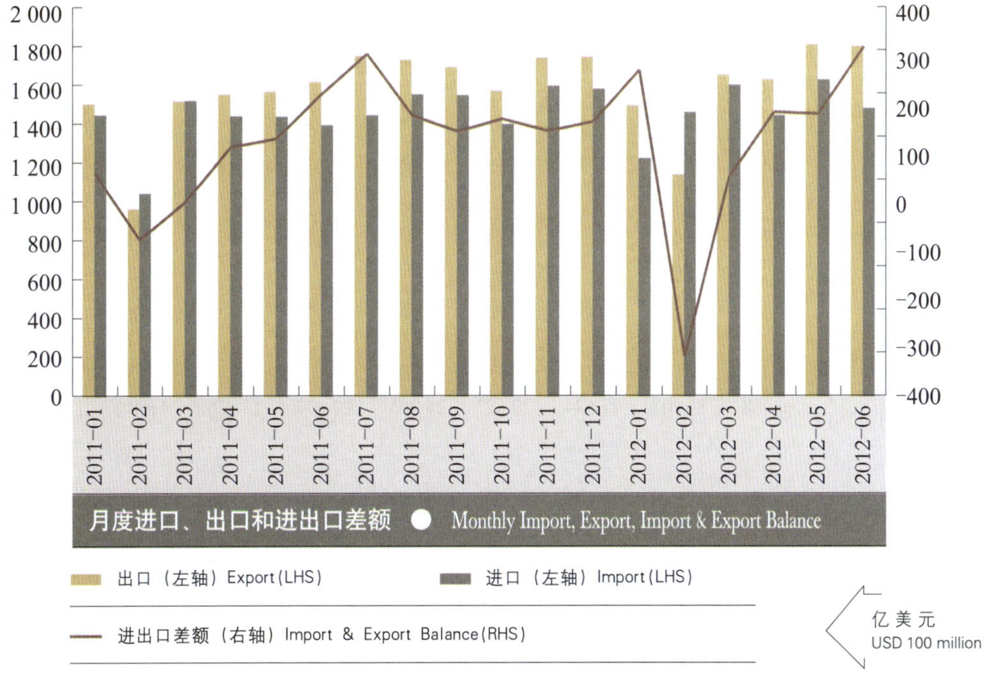

月度进口、出口和进出口差额 ● Monthly Import, Export, Import & Export Balance

按贸易方式分类进出口

Import & Export by Trading Forms

贸易方式Trading Forms	2003	2004	2005	2006	2007	2008	2009	2010	2011	2012H1
进口Import	**412 836**	**561 423**	**660 118**	**791 614**	**955 818**	**1 133 086**	**1 005 555**	**1 394 829**	**1 743 458**	**885 464**
一般贸易 Ordinary Trade	187 700	248 227	279 719	333 181	428 648	572 677	533 872	767 978	1 007 464	514 515
国家间、国际组织间无偿援助和捐赠的物资 Foreign Aid and Donation by Overseas	114	98	49	65	35	49	43	22	16	8
其他捐赠物资 Other Donations	21	12	19	22	10	58	136	185	266	215
来料加工装配贸易 Processing and Assembling Trade	39 125	53 721	67 029	73 834	89 165	90 162	75 993	99 295	93 635	41 925
进料加工贸易 Processing with Imported Materials	123 810	168 020	206 997	247 662	279 228	288 243	246 345	318 134	376 161	185 956
寄售代销贸易 Goods on Consignment	6	8	6	3	2	2	2	2	2	1
边境小额贸易 Border Trade	4 303	5 043	5 721	6 214	7 589	8 975	7 196	9 634	14 448	6 568
加工贸易进口设备 Equipment Imported for Processing & Assembling	1 961	2 603	2 862	2 817	3 277	2 859	953	1 212	885	517
租赁贸易 Goods on Lease	1 392	2 223	3 681	8 067	8 280	6 932	3 448	5 628	5 459	2 844
外商投资企业作为投资进口的设备物品 Equipment or Materials Imported as Investment by Foreign-invested Enterprises	20 968	31 203	27 674	27 823	25 906	27 677	15 176	16 312	17 508	6 984
出料加工贸易 Outward Processing Trade	23	24	33	33	39	160	78	126	73	113
易货贸易 Barter Trade	6	13	3	6	4	1	8	1	2	0
免税外汇商品 Duty Free Commodities on Payment of Foreign Exchange	7	6	8	6	6	6	5	10	13	11
保税仓库进出境货物 Customs Warehousing Trade	7 185	11 081	20 065	32 018	41 720	57 277	54 392	61 099	79 658	42 806
保税仓储转口货物 Entrepot Trade by Bonded Area	25 147	37 720	44 255	55 508	66 910	73 739	64 259	109 241	140 831	79 194

单位：百万美元
Unit: USD million

贸易方式Trading Forms	2003	2004	2005	2006	2007	2008	2009	2010	2011	2012H1
出口加工区进口设备 Equipment Imported into Export Processing Zone	558	882	1 411	3 623	4 108	3 118	2 113	3 994	4 741	2 668
其他Others	510	539	586	732	890	1 150	1 535	1 957	2 296	1 140
出口Export	**438 371**	**593 368**	**761 999**	**969 073**	**1 218 015**	**1 428 546**	**1 201 663**	**1 577 932**	**1 898 600**	**954 376**
一般贸易 Ordinary Trade	182 034	243 635	315 091	416 318	538 576	662 584	529 833	720 733	917 124	460 576
国家间、国际组织间无偿援助和捐赠的物资 Foreign Aid and Donation by Overseas	106	187	225	211	201	231	291	294	471	290
其他捐赠物资Other Donations	0	0	0	0	0	2	8	3	11	1
补偿贸易 Compensation Trade	17	9	0	1	0	0	0	0	0	0
来料加工装配贸易 Processing and Assembling Trade	54 332	68 569	83 970	94 483	116 043	110 520	93 423	112 317	107 653	46 930
进料加工贸易 Processing with Imported Materials	187 517	259 419	332 511	415 892	501 613	564 663	493 558	628 017	727 763	368 338
寄售代销贸易 Goods on Consignment	1	1	1	2	4	4	6	1	2	4
边境小额贸易 Border Trade	3 476	4 431	7 409	9 943	13 739	21 904	13 667	16 408	20 203	9 374
对外承包工程出口货物 Contracting Projects	640	1 130	1 705	3 071	5 188	10 963	13 357	12 617	14 923	6 836
租赁贸易 Goods on Lease	8	15	90	214	84	189	117	145	166	113
出料加工贸易 Outward Processing Trade	20	27	27	24	44	118	46	185	198	99
易货贸易 Barter Trade	41	28	17	19	48	16	1	1	1	0
保税仓库进出境货物 Customs Warehousing Trade	4 017	5 739	7 956	13 069	18 624	28 404	26 793	35 366	43 294	20 263
保税仓储转口货物 Entrepot Trade by Bonded Area	5 488	9 354	11 615	14 463	20 977	23 937	21 476	36 502	49 655	32 761
其他Others	674	824	1 380	1 361	2 916	5 011	9 088	15 343	17 135	8 791

按企业类型分类进出口

Import & Export by Type of Enterprises

单位：亿美元
Unit: USD 100 million

企业类型Type of Enterprises	2003	2004	2005	2006	2007	2008	2009	2010	2011	2012H1
进口Import	**4 128**	**5 614**	**6 601**	**7 916**	**9 558**	**11 331**	**10 056**	**13 948**	**17 435**	**8 855**
国有企业 State-owned Enterprises	1 425	1 765	1 972	2 252	2 697	3 538	2 885	3 876	4 934	2 553
外商投资企业 Foreign-funded Enterprises	2 319	3 246	3 875	4 726	5 594	6 200	5 452	7 380	8 648	4 191
中外合作 Sino-foreign Contractual Joint Ventures	100	107	96	99	88	88	66	74	86	41
中外合资 Sino-foreign Equity Joint Ventures	809	1 092	1 184	1 356	1 549	1 818	1 586	2 095	2 561	1 306
外商独资 Foreign Investment Enterprises	1 411	2 046	2 595	3 270	3 957	4 294	3 799	5 212	6 002	2 844
集体企业 Collective Enterprises	132	177	205	200	232	289	265	349	407	186
其他 Other Enterprises	252	427	549	738	1 035	1 304	1 454	2 343	3 445	1 924
出口Export	**4 384**	**5 934**	**7 620**	**9 691**	**12 180**	**14 285**	**12 017**	**15 779**	**18 986**	**9 544**
国有企业 State-owned Enterprises	1 380	1 536	1 688	1 913	2 248	2 572	1 910	2 344	2 672	1 241
外商投资企业 Foreign-funded Enterprises	2 403	3 386	4 442	5 638	6 955	7 906	6 722	8 623	9 953	4 909
中外合作 Sino-foreign Contractual Joint Ventures	132	148	157	177	181	183	146	165	177	78
中外合资 Sino-foreign Equity Joint Ventures	810	1 096	1 360	1 638	1 988	2 269	1 824	2 376	2 731	1 402
外商独资 Foreign Investment Enterprises	1 461	2 142	2 925	3 824	4 786	5 454	4 752	6 082	7 046	3 428
集体企业 Collective Enterprises	251	318	365	411	469	547	405	499	554	251
其他 Other Enterprises	349	694	1 125	1 728	2 508	3 260	2 979	4 314	5 807	3 143
差额Balance	**255**	**319**	**1 019**	**1 775**	**2 622**	**2 955**	**1 961**	**1 831**	**1 551**	**689**
国有企业 State-owned Enterprises	−44	−229	−284	−339	−449	−966	−975	−1 532	−2 262	−1 312
外商投资企业 Foreign-funded Enterprises	84	140	567	912	1 361	1 706	1 270	1 243	1 305	718
中外合作 Sino-foreign Contractual Joint Ventures	33	40	61	78	93	95	80	91	91	38
中外合资 Sino-foreign Equity Joint Ventures	2	4	176	281	439	451	238	281	170	96
外商独资 Foreign Investment Enterprises	50	96	330	553	829	1 160	953	870	1 044	584
集体企业 Collective Enterprises	119	141	160	211	237	258	140	150	147	65
其他 Other Enterprises	97	267	576	990	1 473	1 956	1 525	1 971	2 362	1 219

2012年上半年按贸易方式分类的进口构成
Components of Import by Trading Forms in the First Half of 2012

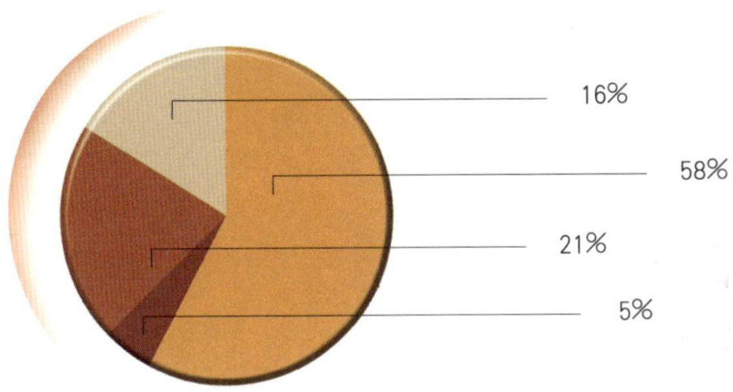

一般贸易 Ordinary Trade
来料加工 Processing with Supplied Materials
进料加工 Processing with Imported Materials
其他 Other Trading Forms

2012年上半年按贸易方式分类的出口构成
Components of Export by Trading Forms in the First Half of 2012

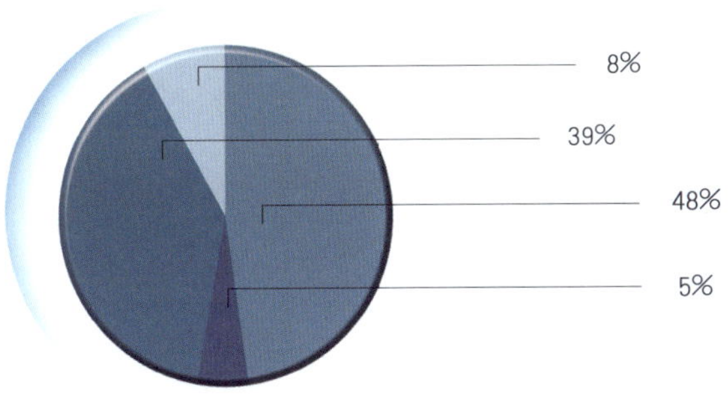

一般贸易 Ordinary Trade
来料加工 Processing with Supplied Materials
进料加工 Processing with Imported Materials
其他 Other Trading Forms

2012年上半年按企业类型分类的进口构成

Components of Import by Type of Enterprises in the First Half of 2012

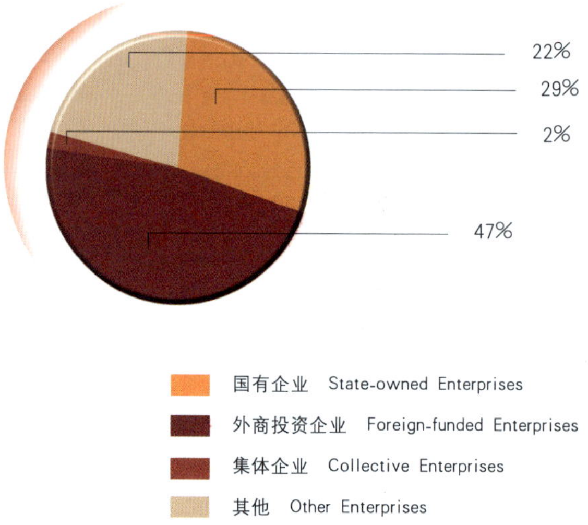

2012年上半年按企业类型分类的出口构成

Components of Export by Type of Enterprises in the First Half of 2012

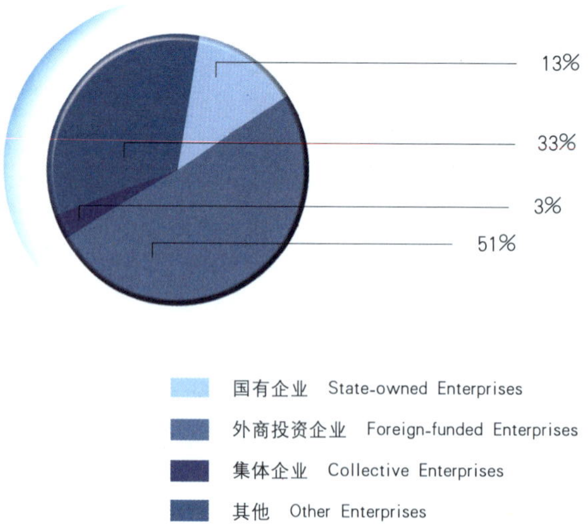

2012年上半年进出口按贸易方式分类

单位：亿美元
Unit: USD 100 million

Import & Export by Trading Forms in the First Half of 2012

贸易方式 Trading Forms	进口 金额Value	Import 同比（%）Increase	出口 金额Value	Export 同比（%）Increase	进出口差额 Import & Export Balance
总值 Total Value	**8 855**	**6.8**	**9 544**	**9.2**	**689**
一般贸易 Ordinary Trade	5 145	8.0	4 606	10.0	–539
加工贸易 Processing Trade	2 279	0.8	4 153	6.4	1 874
来料加工 with Supplied Material	419	−12.0	469	−11.0	50
进料加工 with Imported Material	1 860	4.1	3 684	9.0	1 824
其他贸易 Other Trading Forms	1 431	13.0	785	20.6	−646

2012年上半年进出口按企业类型分类

单位：亿美元
Unit: USD 100 million

Import & Export by Type of Enterprises in the First Half of 2012

企业类型 Type of Enterprises	进口 Import 金额Value	进口 Import 同比（%）Increase	出口 Export 金额Value	出口 Export 同比（%）Increase	进出口差额 Import & Export Balance
总值 Total Value	**8 855**	**6.8**	**9 544**	**9.2**	**689**
国有企业 State-owned Enterprises	2 553	6.8	1 241	−2.4	−1 312
外资企业 Foreign-funded Enterprises	4 191	1.8	4 909	6.0	718
集体企业 Collective Enterprises	186	−6.5	251	−4.9	38
其他企业 Other Enterprises	1 925	21.3	3 143	22.1	96

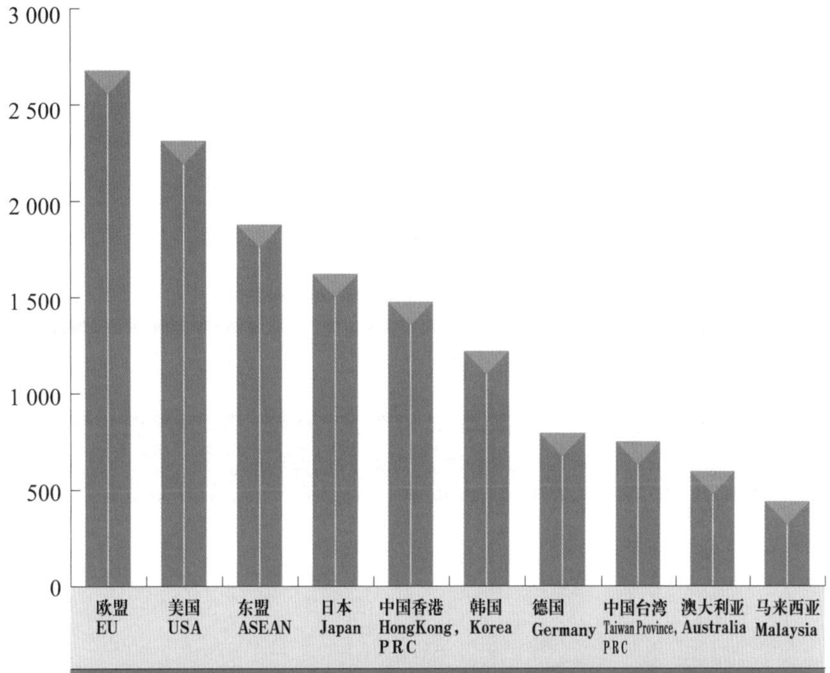

2012年上半年前十位贸易伙伴（按进出口总值）
Top 10 Trading Partners in the First Half of 2012 (Based on the Total Value of Import & Export)

亿美元
USD 100 million

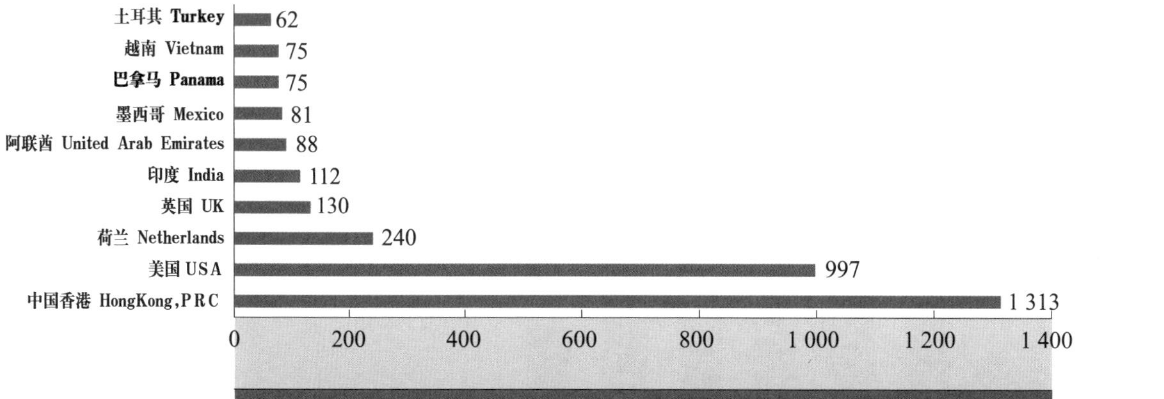

2012年上半年前十位贸易顺差来源地
Top 10 Sources of Trade Surplus in the First Half of 2012

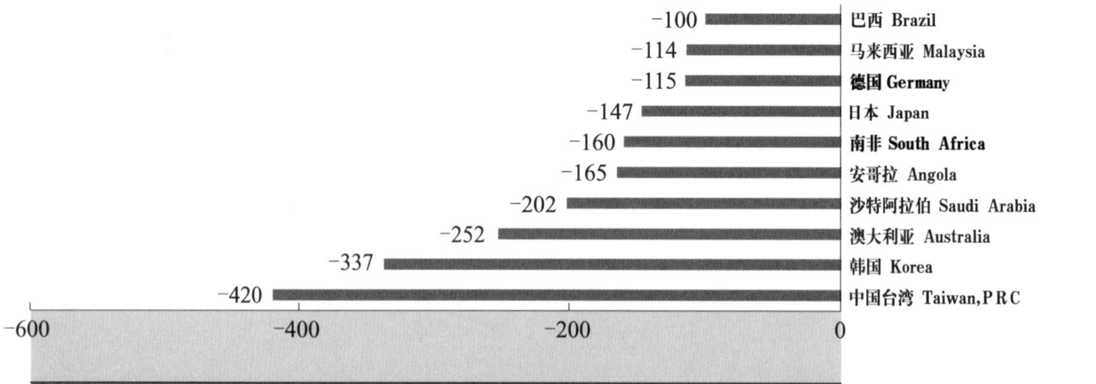

2012年上半年前十位贸易逆差来源地
Top 10 Sources of Trade Deficit in the First Half of 2012

三、外汇市场和人民币汇率①

Ⅲ. Foreign Exchange Market and Exchange Rate of RMB

人民币对美元交易中间价月平均汇价

Monthly Average Transaction Mid Rates of RMB against USD, 1980—2011

人民币元/100美元
RMB per 100 USD

年份year / 月份Month	1980	1981	1982	1983	1984	1985	1986	1987	1988	1989
1月/Jan.	149.37	154.87	176.77	192.01	204.12	280.88	320.15	372.21	372.21	372.21
2月/Feb.	150.05	161.06	181.74	196.03	205.72	282.51	320.70	372.21	372.21	372.21
3月/Mar.	155.12	162.80	183.79	197.80	206.08	284.51	321.20	372.21	372.21	372.21
4月/Apr.	155.70	166.20	185.19	198.72	208.91	284.11	320.61	372.21	372.21	372.21
5月/May	149.06	172.27	180.97	198.52	218.21	284.75	319.44	372.21	372.21	372.21
6月/Jun.	146.50	176.05	189.70	198.95	221.22	286.25	320.35	372.21	372.21	372.21
7月/Jul.	145.25	175.98	192.36	198.88	229.39	287.38	363.82	372.21	372.21	372.21
8月/Aug.	147.26	179.52	193.87	198.00	236.43	290.23	370.36	372.21	372.21	372.21
9月/Sept.	146.81	175.01	195.04	198.14	253.26	296.26	370.66	372.21	372.21	372.21
10月/Oct.	148.03	175.05	198.22	196.17	264.00	306.73	371.64	372.21	372.21	372.21
11月/Nov.	151.73	173.46	199.41	198.90	266.16	320.15	372.21	372.21	372.21	372.21
12月/Dec.	154.19	173.78	193.99	198.69	278.91	320.15	372.21	372.21	372.21	423.82
年平均 Annual Average	**149.84**	**170.50**	**189.25**	**197.57**	**232.70**	**293.66**	**345.28**	**372.21**	**372.21**	**376.51**

①资料来源：国家外汇管理局。
Sources: State Administration of Foreign Exchange.

人民币对美元交易中间价月平均汇价

Monthly Average Transaction Mid Rates of RMB against USD, 1980—2011

人民币元/100美元
RMB per 100 USD

年份year / 月份Month	1990	1991	1992	1993	1994	1995	1996	1997	1998	1999	2000
1 月/Jan.	472.21	522.21	544.81	576.40	870.00	844.13	831.86	829.63	827.91	827.90	827.93
2 月/Feb.	472.21	522.21	546.35	576.99	870.28	843.54	831.32	829.29	827.91	827.80	827.79
3 月/Mar.	472.21	522.21	547.34	573.13	870.23	842.76	832.89	829.57	827.92	827.91	827.86
4 月/Apr.	472.21	526.59	549.65	570.63	869.55	842.25	833.15	829.57	827.92	827.92	827.93
5 月/May	472.21	531.39	550.36	572.17	866.49	831.28	832.88	829.29	827.90	827.85	827.77
6 月/Jun.	472.21	535.35	547.51	573.74	865.72	830.08	832.26	829.21	827.97	827.80	827.72
7 月/Jul.	472.21	535.55	544.32	576.12	864.03	830.07	831.60	829.11	827.98	827.77	827.93
8 月/Aug.	472.21	537.35	542.87	577.64	858.98	830.75	830.81	828.94	827.99	827.73	827.96
9 月/Sept.	472.21	537.35	549.48	578.70	854.03	831.88	830.44	828.72	827.89	827.74	827.86
10 月/Oct.	472.21	537.90	553.69	578.68	852.93	831.55	830.00	828.38	827.78	827.74	827.85
11月/Nov.	495.54	538.58	561.31	579.47	851.69	831.35	829.93	828.11	827.78	827.82	827.74
12月/Dec.	522.21	541.31	579.82	580.68	848.45	831.56	829.90	827.96	827.79	827.93	827.72
年平均 Annual Average	**478.32**	**532.33**	**551.46**	**576.20**	**861.87**	**835.10**	**831.42**	**828.98**	**827.91**	**827.83**	**827.84**

人民币对美元交易中间价月平均汇价

人民币元/100美元
RMB per 100 USD

Monthly Average Transaction Mid Rates of RMB against USD, 1980—2011

年份year / 月份Month	2001	2002	2003	2004	2005	2006	2007	2008	2009	2010	2011
1月/Jan.	827.71	827.67	827.68	827.69	827.65	806.68	778.98	724.78	683.82	682.73	660.27
2月/Feb.	827.70	827.66	827.73	827.71	827.65	804.93	775.46	716.01	683.57	682.7	658.31
3月/Mar.	827.76	827.70	827.72	827.71	827.65	803.50	773.90	707.52	683.41	682.64	656.62
4月/Apr.	827.71	827.72	827.71	827.69	827.65	801.56	772.47	700.07	683.12	682.62	652.92
5月/May	827.72	827.69	827.69	827.71	827.65	801.52	767.04	697.24	682.45	682.74	649.88
6月/Jun.	827.71	827.70	827.71	827.67	827.65	800.67	763.30	689.71	683.32	681.65	647.78
7月/Jul.	827.69	827.68	827.73	827.67	822.90	799.10	758.05	683.76	683.20	677.75	646.14
8月/Aug.	827.70	827.67	827.70	827.68	810.19	797.33	757.53	685.15	683.22	679.01	640.9
9月/Sept.	827.68	827.70	827.71	827.67	809.22	793.68	752.58	683.07	682.89	674.62	638.33
10月/Oct.	827.68	827.69	827.67	827.65	808.89	790.32	750.12	683.16	682.75	667.32	635.66
11月/Nov.	827.69	827.71	827.69	827.65	808.40	786.52	742.33	682.86	682.74	665.58	634.08
12月/Dec.	827.68	827.72	827.70	827.65	807.59	782.38	736.76	684.24	682.79	665.15	632.81
年平均 Annual Average	**827.70**	**827.70**	**827.70**	**827.68**	**819.17**	**797.18**	**760.40**	**694.51**	**683.10**	**676.95**	**646.14**

2012年1–6月人民币市场汇率汇总表

林吉特、卢布单位：外币/100人民币
其他7种币种单位：人民币元/100外币
MYR, RUB Unit: foreign currency per 100 RMB
Other 7 Currency unit: RMB per 100 foreign currency

Transaction Mid Rates of RMB in the First Half of 2012

月份Month	币种 Currency	期初价 Beginning of Period	期末价 End of Period	最高价 Highest	最低价 Lowest	期平均 Period Average	累计平均 Accumulative Average
1月 Jan.	美元 USD	630.01	631.15	633.06	630.01	631.68	631.68
	港币 HKD	81.112	81.363	81.497	81.112	81.352	81.352
	日元 JPY	8.2198	8.2649	8.2649	8.1816	8.2213	8.2213
	欧元 EUR	822.04	830.06	831.99	801.04	811.78	811.78
	英镑 GBP	985.37	992.01	992.01	968.52	977.36	977.36
	澳元 AUD	652.19	670.22	670.22	642.60	654.18	654.18
	加元 CAD	622.39	630.36	630.36	613.76	621.94	621.94
	林吉特 MYR	49.851	48.372	50.087	48.191	49.447	49.447
	卢布 RUB	503.83	481.15	507.50	477.20	499.12	499.12
2月 Feb.	美元 USD	631.03	629.19	631.16	629.19	630.00	630.70
	港币 HKD	81.359	81.132	81.397	81.132	81.241	81.287
	日元 JPY	8.2796	7.8107	8.2846	7.7534	8.0409	8.1161
	欧元 EUR	825.36	847.99	847.99	821.37	833.12	824.23
	英镑 GBP	994.31	1 001.83	1 001.91	987.10	995.21	987.77
	澳元 AUD	669.24	679.78	679.97	669.20	675.41	666.56
	加元 CAD	629.30	633.08	634.68	628.87	631.50	627.52
	林吉特 MYR	48.137	47.626	48.443	47.626	48.007	48.607
	卢布 RUB	479.71	460.18	481.45	457.72	473.00	483.88
3月 Mar.	美元 USD	630.16	629.43	633.59	628.40	630.81	630.74
	港币 HKD	81.251	81.063	81.616	80.893	81.268	81.280
	日元 JPY	7.7630	7.6690	7.8287	7.5419	7.6487	7.9388
	欧元 EUR	840.16	839.44	840.16	824.90	833.69	827.82
	英镑 GBP	1 003.56	1 005.42	1 005.42	989.47	998.33	991.78
	澳元 AUD	676.32	654.04	679.62	652.83	665.04	665.98
	加元 CAD	637.43	631.67	640.19	629.45	635.23	630.44
	林吉特 MYR	47.690	48.709	48.899	47.589	48.228	48.463
	卢布 RUB	462.86	467.49	469.29	457.88	464.83	476.65
4月 Apr.	美元 USD	630.35	627.87	630.72	627.87	629.66	630.50
	港币 HKD	81.173	80.922	81.232	80.922	81.120	81.244
	日元 JPY	7.6541	7.7362	7.8127	7.6541	7.7408	7.8939
	欧元 EUR	828.50	829.32	831.05	819.39	827.03	827.64
	英镑 GBP	1 002.19	1 015.99	1 015.99	996.44	1 006.34	995.08
	澳元 AUD	647.53	651.51	656.77	645.90	650.78	662.54
	加元 CAD	632.37	637.37	638.86	626.98	633.36	631.10
	林吉特 MYR	48.631	48.500	48.821	48.500	48.654	48.507
	卢布 RUB	467.64	466.34	472.44	465.75	468.38	474.78
5月 May.	美元 USD	626.70	633.55	633.55	626.70	630.62	630.53
	港币 HKD	80.784	81.583	81.583	80.784	81.224	81.239
	日元 JPY	7.8089	8.0293	8.0293	7.8089	7.9047	7.8964
	欧元 EUR	828.59	783.51	828.59	783.51	807.15	822.99
	英镑 GBP	1 016.79	980.10	1 016.79	980.10	1 004.30	997.17
	澳元 AUD	647.54	614.13	647.54	614.13	628.89	654.91
	加元 CAD	635.63	615.10	635.74	615.10	624.63	629.63
	林吉特 MYR	48.156	50.246	50.246	48.156	49.099	48.641
	卢布 RUB	467.09	517.43	517.43	467.09	488.41	477.87
6月 Jun.	美元 USD	633.08	632.49	633.08	630.04	631.78	630.74
	港币 HKD	81.549	81.522	81.574	81.199	81.423	81.271
	日元 JPY	8.0686	7.9648	8.0970	7.8400	7.9733	7.9095
	欧元 EUR	781.51	787.10	801.05	781.51	792.10	817.71
	英镑 GBP	974.18	981.69	990.30	971.16	981.99	994.57
	澳元 AUD	613.99	634.74	642.22	609.41	629.34	650.54
	加元 CAD	611.91	612.23	618.58	605.86	614.58	627.06
	林吉特 MYR	50.307	50.535	50.676	49.828	50.289	48.923
	卢布 RUB	526.05	523.34	530.97	510.12	518.25	484.77

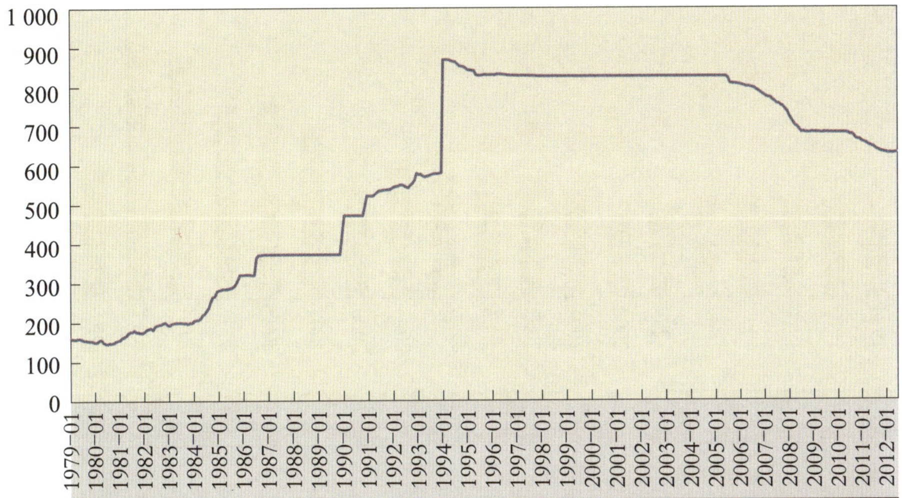

1979—2012年上半年人民币对美元交易中间价月平均汇价

Monthly Average Transaction Mid Rates of RMB Against USD, 1979–Jun.2012

人民币元/100美元
RMB per 100 USD

四、利用外资①

Ⅳ. Foreign Investment Utilization

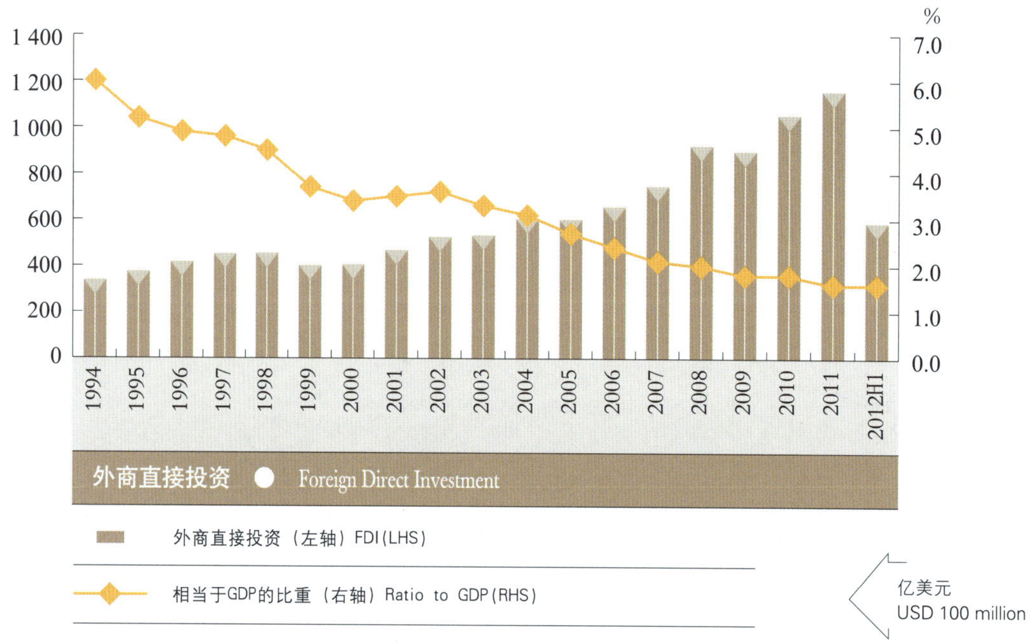

①资料来源：商务部。
Sources：Ministry of Commerce.

2012年上半年利用外资

单位：亿美元
Unit: USD 100 million

Foreign Direct Investment in the First Half of 2012

利用外资方式 Mode of Foreign Investment Utilization	本年批准外资项目数 Approved Foreign Investment Programs		本年实际使用外资 Actual Utilization of Foreign Investment	
	本年累计 Accumulative in This Year	同比增长(%) Increase	本年累计 Accumulative in This Year	同比增长(%) Increase
总计 Total	**11 705**	**−13.05**	**597.33**	**−3.3**
一、外商直接投资 Direct Foreign Investment	11 705	−13.05	590.89	−2.96
中外合资企业 Sino-Foreign Equity Joint Venture	2 024	−16.16	122.97	14.26
中外合作企业 Sino-Foreign Contractual Joint Venture	84	−45.1	10.11	13.29
外资企业 Foreign Investment Enterprise	9 570	−12.02	450.87	−6.71
外商投资股份制 Stock-Holding by Foreign Investment	27	58.82	6.94	−23.21
合作开发 Cooperation Exploitation	0		0	
其他 Others	0		0	
二、外商其他投资 Other Foreign Investment	0		6.44	−26.79
对外发行股票 Issue Stocks to the Outside	0		3.77	−24.84
国际租赁 International Tenancy	0		0	
补偿贸易 Compensative Trade	0		0	−100
加工装配 Processing & amp; Assembling	0		2.67	−24.06

注：统计数据为非金融领域。
Note: The data is subject to non-financial sectors.

五、外债①

V. External Debt

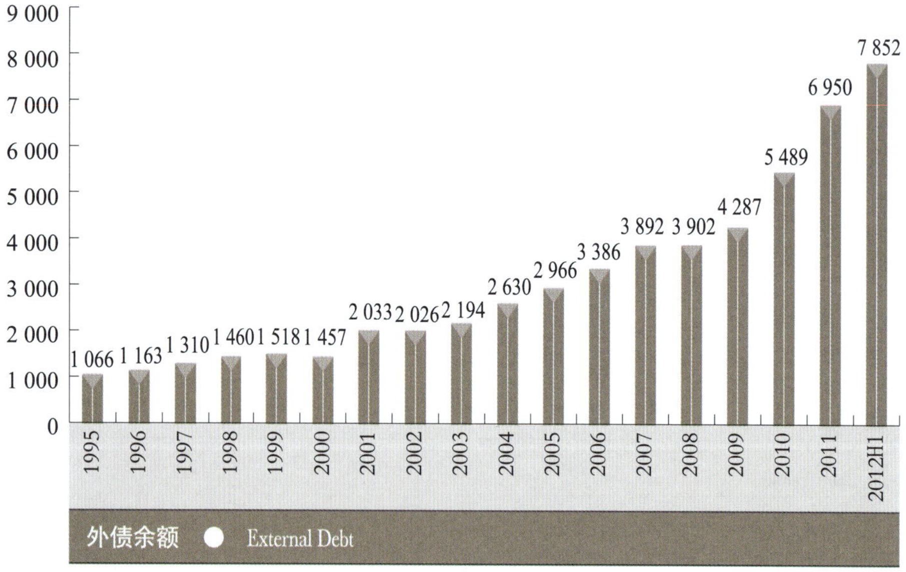

亿美元
USD 100 million

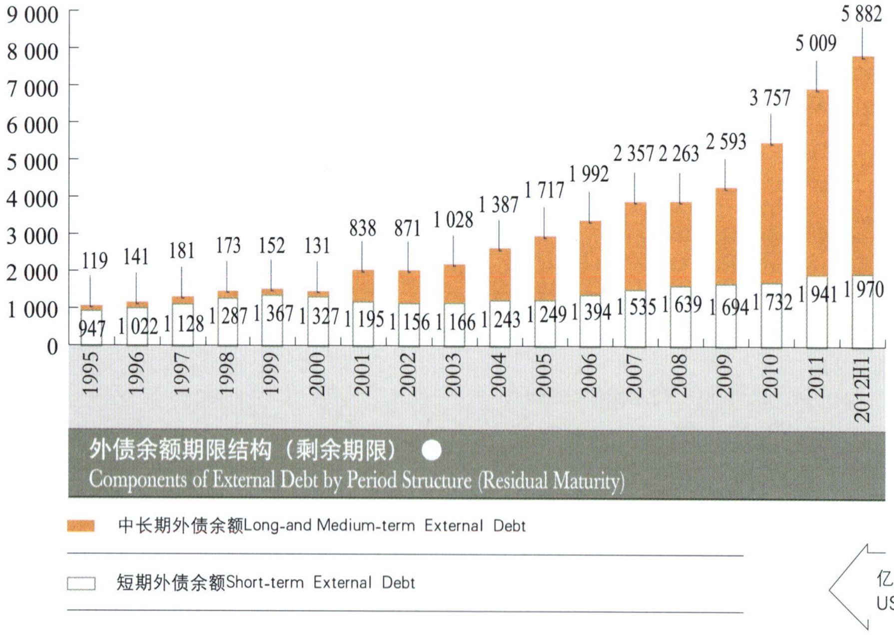

亿美元
USD 100 million

①资料来源：国家外汇管理局。
Sources：State Administration of Foreign Exchange.

2012年6月末外债余额期限结构（剩余期限）
Components of External Debt by Period Structure (Residual Maturity), End of Jun.2012

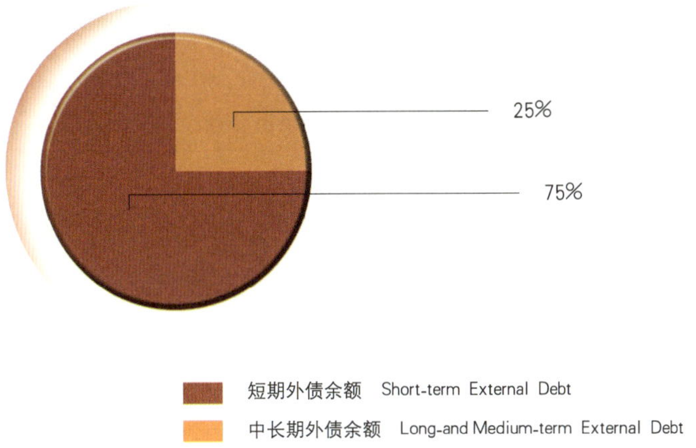

2012年6月末登记外债余额主体结构
Components of Registered External Debt by Type of Debtor, End of Jun.2012

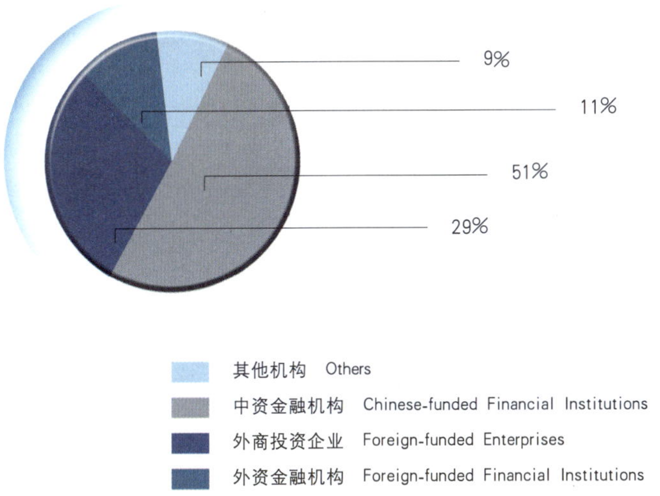

六、国际旅游[①]

Ⅵ. International Tourism

入境过夜旅游者人数和旅游外汇收入

Number of Inbound Stay-over Tourists and Foreign Exchange Income from Tourism

年份 Year	入境过夜旅游（万人次） Inbound Stay-over Tourists(10 000 persons)	旅游外汇收入（亿美元） Foreign Exchange Income from Tourism(USD 100 million)	年份 Year	入境过夜旅游（万人次） Inbound Stay-over Tourists(10 000 persons)	旅游外汇收入（亿美元） Foreign Exchange Income from Tourism(USD 100 million)
1978	71.6	2.63	1996	2 276.5	102.00
1979	152.9	4.49	1997	2 377.0	120.74
1980	350.0	6.17	1998	2 507.3	126.02
1981	367.7	7.85	1999	2 704.7	140.99
1982	392.4	8.43	2000	3 122.9	162.24
1983	379.1	9.41	2001	3 316.7	177.92
1984	514.1	11.31	2002	3 680.3	203.85
1985	713.3	12.50	2003	3 297.1	174.06
1986	900.1	15.31	2004	4 176.1	257.39
1987	1 076.0	18.62	2005	4 680.9	292.96
1988	1 236.1	22.47	2006	4 991.0	339.49
1989	936.1	18.60	2007	5 472.0	419.19
1990	1 048.4	22.18	2008	5 304.9	408.43
1991	1 246.4	28.45	2009	5 087.5	396.75
1992	1 651.2	39.47	2010	5 566.5	519.75
1993	1 898.2	46.83	2011	5 758.1	596.82
1994	2 107.0	73.23	2012H1	2 824.5	238.28
1995	2 003.4	87.33			

①资料来源：国家旅游局。
Sources：China National Tourism Administration.

七、世界经济增长状况①

Ⅶ. Growth of World Economy

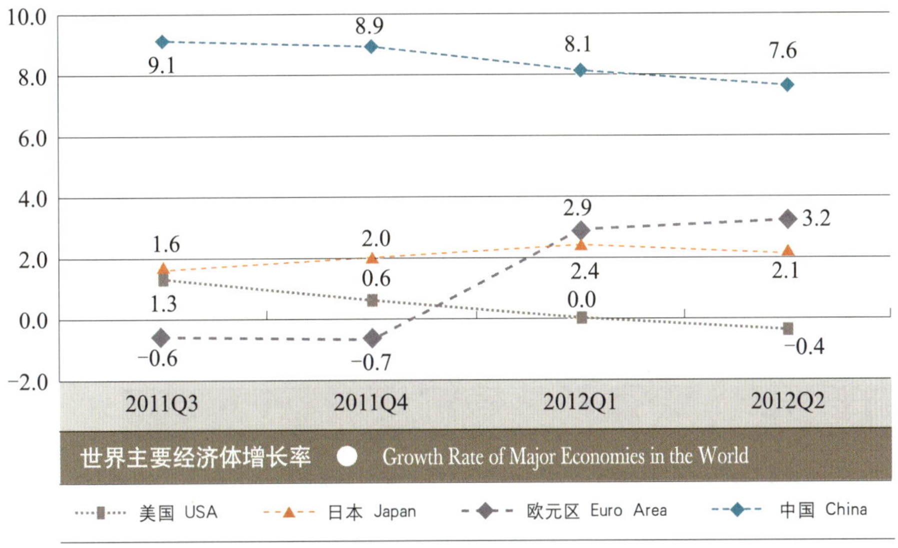

经济增长率 (%)
Growth Rate of Economy (%)

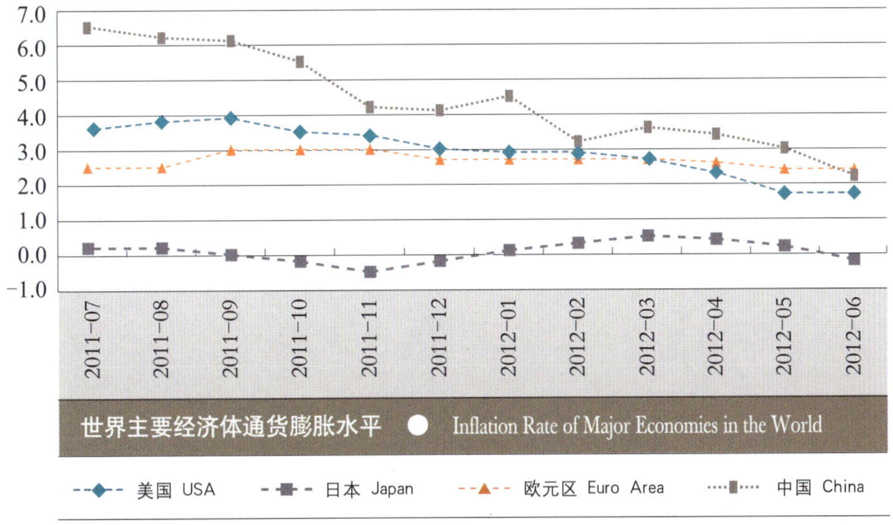

居民消费价格指数
CPI（%）

①资料来源：彭博资讯；CEIC Asia Database。
Sources：Bloomberg，CEIC Asia Database.

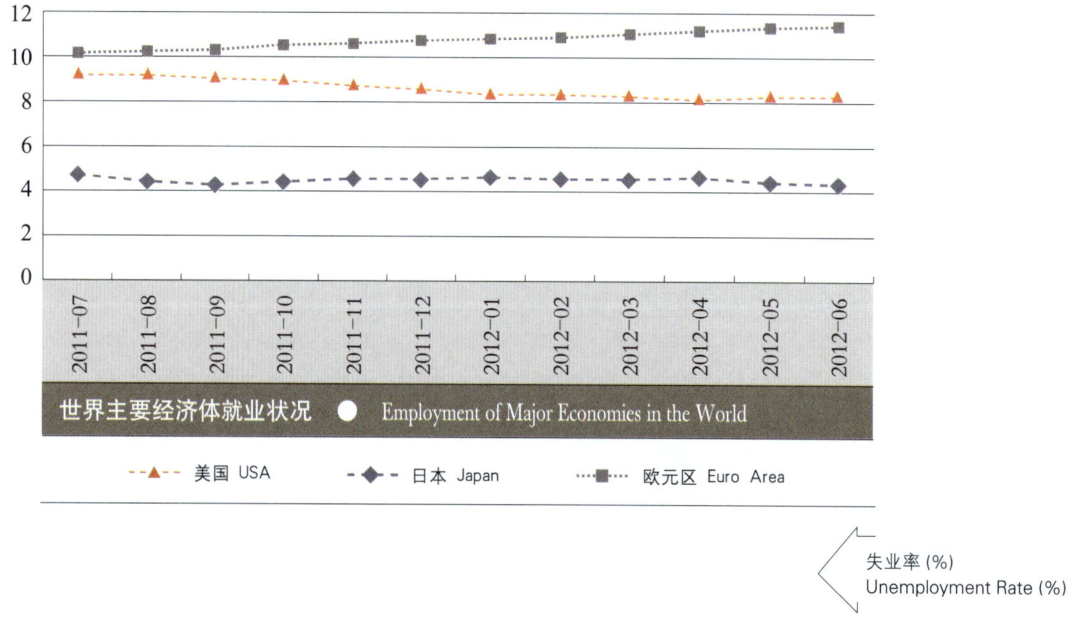

世界主要经济体就业状况 ● Employment of Major Economies in the World

八、国际金融市场状况①

Ⅷ. International Financial Market

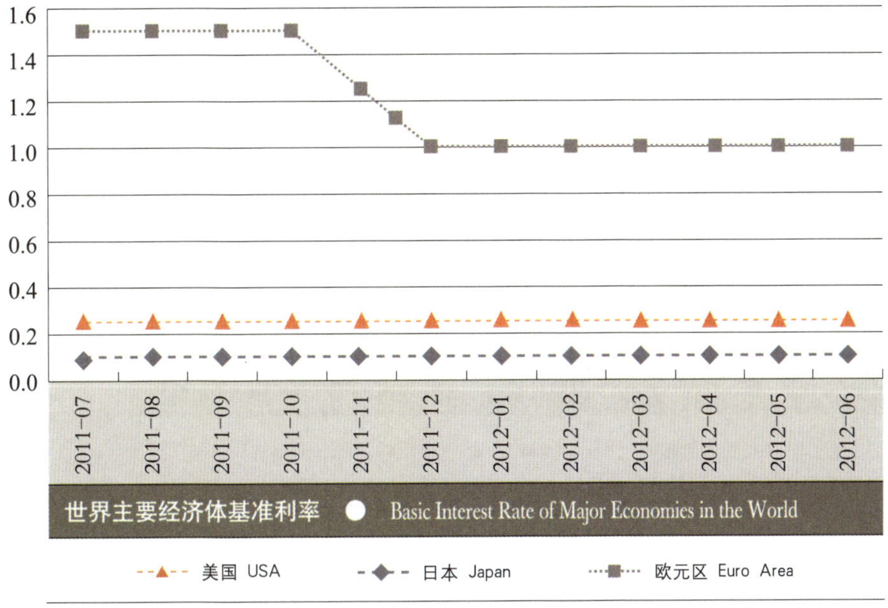

世界主要经济体基准利率 ● Basic Interest Rate of Major Economies in the World

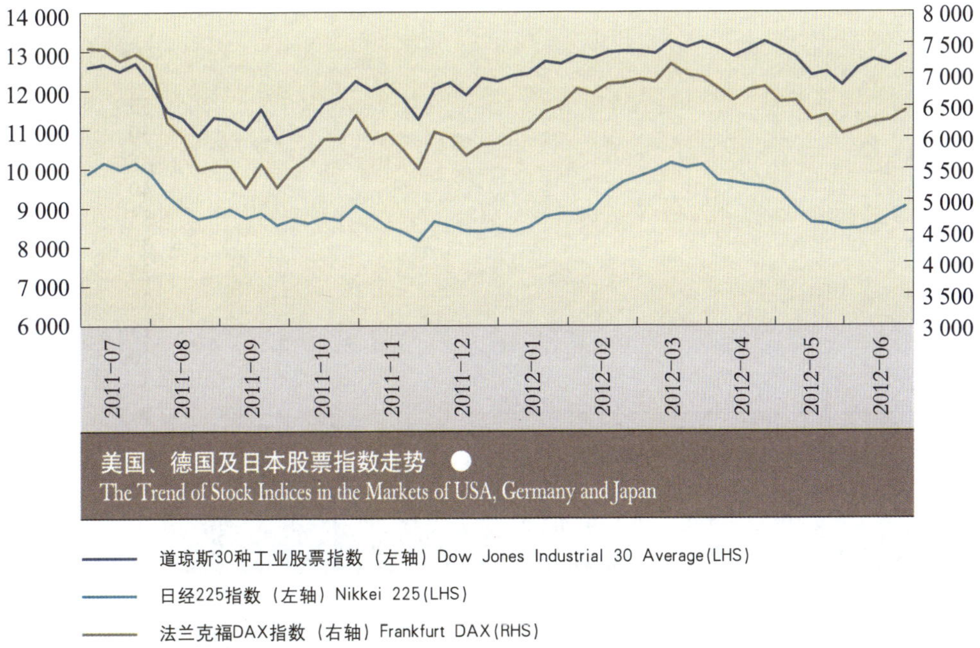

美国、德国及日本股票指数走势 ●
The Trend of Stock Indices in the Markets of USA, Germany and Japan

①资料来源：彭博资讯。
Sources: Bloomberg.

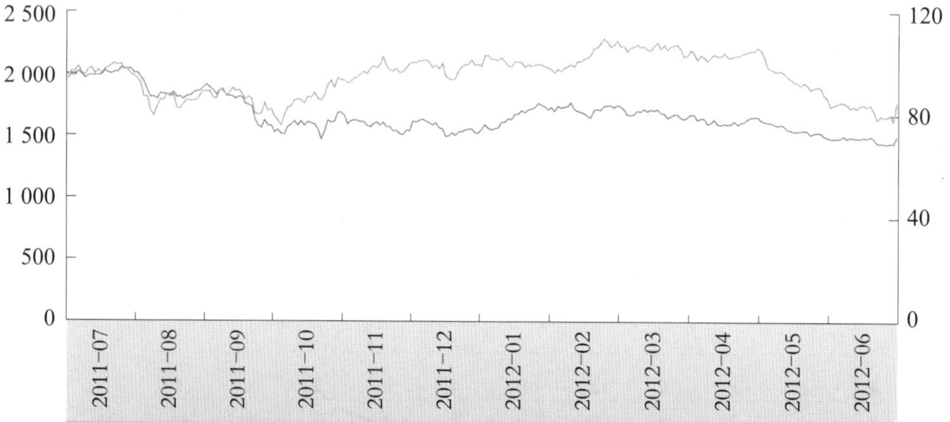

国际商品价格 ● Price of International Commodities

高盛工业金属价格指数（总回报率）（左轴）Goldman Sachs Industrial Metal Index Total Return(LHS)

纽约商品交易所原油期货价格（右轴） NYMEX Crude Oil Future Price(RHS)

美元/桶
USD/Barrel

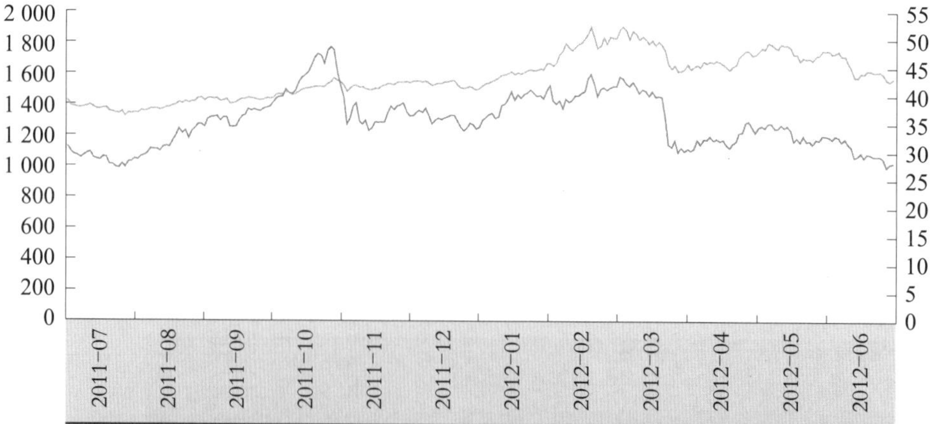

伦敦金属交易所金银价格 ● LME Gold and Silver Price

黄金（左轴）Gold(LHS)

白银（右轴）Silver(RHS)

美元/盎司
USD/Ounce